THE ANXIETY ENCYCLOPEDIA

YOUR PATH TO RECOVERY

JOTHAM SADAN

The Anxiety Encyclopedia: Your Path to Recovery

Copyright © 2020 by Jotham Sadan

All rights reserved.

THE ANXIETY ENCYCLOPEDIA

Contents

Preface

For many of us who have struggled with anxious symptoms, it all started with a panic attack. The adrenaline began pumping through our veins, our heart rate doubled, and our brain tried to tell us we had to get out, to escape some invisible force that was closing in on us. But unlike the other panic attacks, this one would not let up. Minutes turned to hours, then to days and weeks. Our constant worrying about another panic attack forced us to retreat further and further into ourselves. For me, that panic attack was on Tuesday, April 25, 2017, at around 10:00 a.m. This was not the first panic attack I had ever had, but it was the one that marked my transition from stressed out college student to someone who could not eat, drink, or sleep, much less leave the house. Looking back, this panic attack fractured my life into four distinct parts: the years I spent just coping with anxious symptoms; the months of constant panic; the slow, tooth-and-nail climb out; and the eventual freedom from the lifelong shadow that anxious symptoms and excessive worrying cast over me.

If my experience sounds familiar to you, you are not alone. According to the Anxiety and Depression Association of America (ADAA)[1], around 40 million Americans are believed to have trouble with anxious symptoms, ranging from mild to severe, generalized to situation-specific, and mental to physical compulsions. This accounts for an astonishing 18% of the total population—one out of every five people.

For most of us, this is a lonely experience. We might not have the money, time, or access to treatment, and even those of us who do can struggle to see results. Our therapist or mental health professional might be experienced in their field, but they might not know how to treat excessive worrying. Trying to share our complex symptoms with someone who has not experienced them is an exercise in futility.

Worst of all, despite all of the discussion these days, no one has been able to give a satisfying explanation of how anxious symptoms and excessive worrying *actually* work. There is a mountain of research on the effects of environment, genetics, and neurotransmitters, and yet no one has been able to put a finger on what happens when we are anxious and why.

This has led to thousands of treatments—therapies, medications, mineral supplements, exercises, and meditations—but very few are backed by science, and none provide a model that explains exactly why it works.

That was my motivation for writing this book. I wanted to create a single source to bring together all the medical and psychological knowledge we have of anxiety, then use that knowledge to construct a new model that ties it all together—an anxiety encyclopedia. That way, we can build a treatment method that guarantees recovery, no matter how severe the symptoms.

Thank you for reading *The Anxiety Encyclopedia*. Please enjoy.

Introduction

"My heart is beating so fast. Am I having a heart attack?"

"What are all of these weird thoughts? Am I going crazy?"

"My chest feels like it's about to explode. What if I am dying?"

If you have had high anxiety before, these thoughts and symptoms probably sound familiar. On the lower end of the spectrum, anxiety can cause a rise in heart rate, muscle tightness, and dizziness, negatively impacting our life. On the severe end, familiar to far fewer of us, things get a lot scarier. Shortness of breath so intense it feels as if we could faint at any moment. Heart rate nearing its peak without moving a muscle. Nausea strong enough to prevent us from eating for days. Then there are the mental symptoms. The feeling that the world is closing in on us. Dissociation causing us to feel disconnected from our surroundings. Bizarre thoughts about violent, depraved, or nonsensical things that make it seem as if we are losing touch with reality. And sometimes worst of all, the fear that, even in our better moments, it will come back.

I want to start by addressing the question you have probably asked yourself a hundred times: Will this anxiety I am experiencing last forever? The answer, which I say with absolute confidence, is *no*. An anxiety disorder, when treated properly, is nothing more than a temporary period.

Googling "is anxiety curable" will bring up plenty of conflicting answers, with an even split of "yes, anxiety is curable," and "no, it is only manageable." So let me clear things up: the mechanism of anxiety is like the mechanism behind physical pain—a sensation our body makes when it is driven out of equilibrium. When we lift too much weight or run too quickly, pain is our body's way of telling us to slow down. In the same way, when we are in danger or need to focus, anxiety is our body's way of giving us a boost. Since experiencing pain and anxiety in this way can be helpful, they are not something we want to eliminate completely.

However, there are times when our body is driven so far out of equilibrium that these mechanisms bring us great discomfort. Just like we feel overwhelming pain when we maintain bad posture for years, certain behaviors will cause us to experience overwhelming anxious symptoms—symptoms that may come up in random and inappropriate situations (or if you are like I was, all day every day), and far more intensely than those around us.

In these cases, the symptoms are not the problem. Rather, there is a separate problem that *causes* us to experience them. When we work on our posture, doing physical therapy and choosing to sit upright more often, our body gradually returns to normal, and the pain slowly goes away as a result. Anxiety is the same—there are problems that *cause* our body to produce anxious symptoms far more than is necessary. When we address these problems, our body slowly returns to normal, reducing the strength of anxious symptoms until they only pop up occasionally and at low strength. In that sense, anxiety disorders— periods of uncomfortably high anxiety—are *absolutely* curable.

Unfortunately, the discussion around why anxious symptoms happen has become two-sided, with neither side able to put their finger on the issue. On one end, people unfamiliar with anxiety disorders argue that everyone has to deal with the same anxious symptoms, despite never having a panic attack or an episode of depersonalization themselves.

On the opposite end, some argue that these anxious symptoms pop up because of an inescapable genetic or chemical imbalance. Doctors who were never educated on the subject see their patients suffering and rush to help them the only way they know how: medication and management techniques. But this management-focused approach only came about recently. We have known about anxious symptoms for over a hundred years, and up until the 1980s, they were not considered a chronic condition at all. In fact, Claire Weekes, doctor and founder of the most successful treatment to date, argued that management-focused treatments only temporarily dulled anxious symptoms and did nothing to treat the root cause.

As the world has become more demanding, these two mentalities have become dominant; anxious symptoms are treated as either a problem of weak character or an uncontrollable genetic deficiency. And despite how widespread these mindsets have become, leading to breathing techniques and meditation on one end and antidepressants and benzodiazepines on the other, the number of people having trouble is only increasing.[2]

As you will read, all of the different diagnoses we have for anxiety—social anxiety, generalized anxiety, health anxiety, OCD, pure obsession, agoraphobia and other acute and chronic phobias—have a similar mechanism at their core that *causes* these symptoms. One that has nothing to do with weak character or a permanent chemical imbalance and everything to do with our behavior (but not in the traditional sense).

Anxious symptoms and excessive worrying are like many other health problems in this way, especially weight-related diseases like type 2 diabetes. These diseases come with a wide range of symptoms like numbness and fatigue that happen when we have been over-eating for years and our body is no longer able to sustain our diet. When we reach this point, medications like insulin might address the symptoms and can be vital for recovery, but they do nothing to fix the cause of our problem: the unhealthy eating habits we sustain. The approach to anxious symptoms is the same—medications may help dull symptoms in the short term, but if we do not treat the root cause, our symptoms will eventually outpace the medication. The key to both weight-related issues and anxious symptoms, the one that leads to lasting health, is addressing the unhealthy behaviors and letting our body return to normal.

My purpose in writing this book is threefold. First, I will present a new model for anxiety. Second, I use this model to suggest three different therapies for treatment and explain exactly why they work. Last, I use this model to explain why certain lifestyle changes like exercise and meditation can help supplement our recovery and give tips on how to best engage in them. The end goal is for readers—those of us looking to treat ourselves or healthcare practitioners looking to better understand their patients—pave a clear path to recovery. To help others make the same transformation I made, from chronically panicked and symptomatic to freed from both. From simply managing the anxious symptoms to fixing the mechanisms at the core.

* * *

Before we start, I think it is important to discuss exactly how to use this book. My intent in writing this is to gather all the information you might need during recovery from issues with anxious symptoms and excessive worrying: the science, the treatment, the lifestyle changes, and a recovery roadmap.

This book is not meant to be gospel. Though the methods are well established, the way you apply them will be highly personal. This book is meant to serve as a general roadmap for your treatment, one that will point you in the right direction but leave some of the specifics up to you.

Also, though this book contains the tools, it will be up to you to use them. Due to how the brain works, overcoming anxious symptoms and excessive worrying will mean confronting all of the discomfort you may have been trying to avoid. But unlike how you approached things in the past, the knowledge in this book will help you turn formerly negative experiences into positive ones—experiences that help reduce anxious symptoms rather than making them worse. Like finally correcting a lifetime of bad posture, you will give your body the chance to rebuild its muscles rather than continuing to strain them.

If you are skeptical, that is okay. In fact, I think heading into any treatment plan with some skepticism is healthy. However, I ask you to give the theory and methods in this book an honest go for at least three weeks. I am confident that once you begin to see improvement, your trust in yourself and in the methods will grow.

So with all that said, let us start our exploration into anxiety with a look at the mechanism behind it. This will help us answer some of the most common questions we have: Why certain people experience anxious symptoms while others do not. Why some people worry excessively while others never do. How anxious symptoms get worse, leading to panic, phobias, and obsessive compulsions. And finally, how we can use the science behind them to recover.

THE SCIENCE
OF ANXIETY

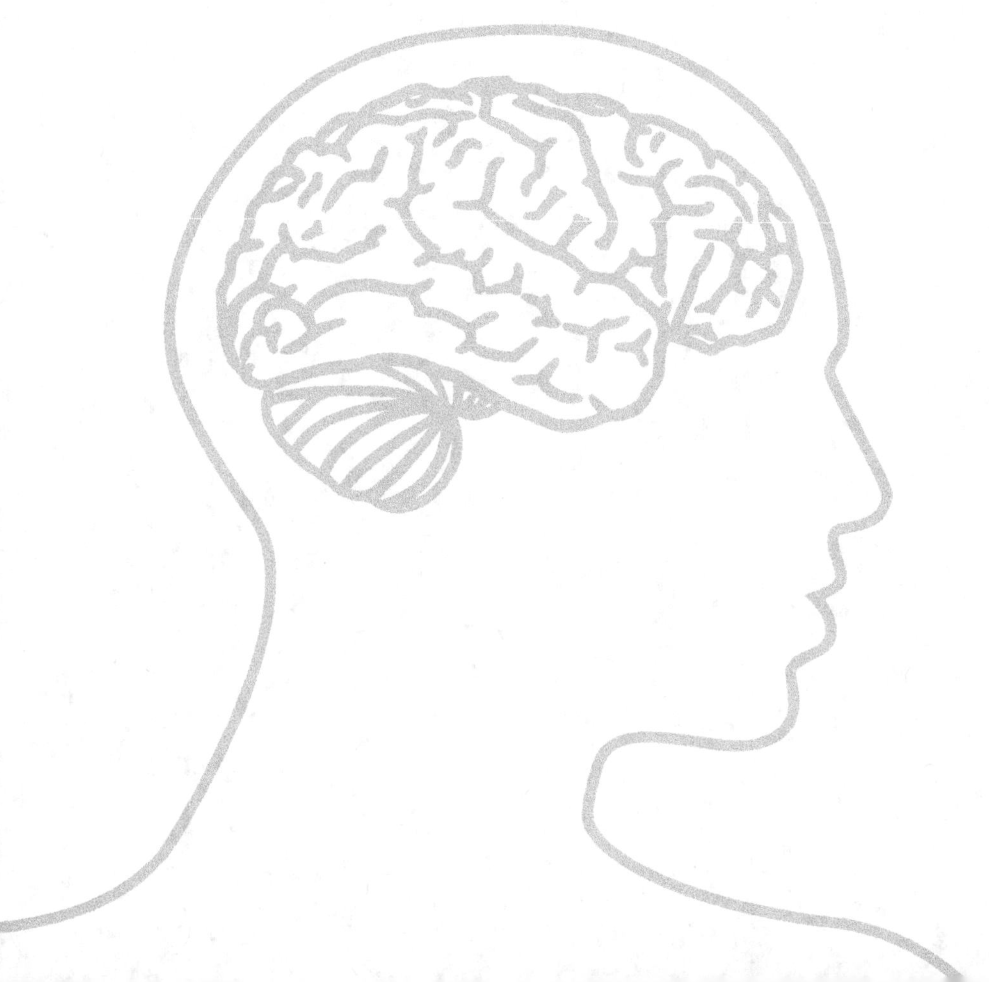

The Biological and Psychological Roots of Anxiety

Before we get into how to treat anxious symptoms, we must first understand how they work. The reason for this is simple but vitally important: all of the therapies we will use build on this understanding. The better our understanding, the more effective these therapies will be.

To understand why our body works the way it does, scientists usually study our evolution. They look at why our ancestors might have needed to be anxious and what role this mechanism is supposed to have in our lives today. For this, the following chapter will help answer the question: what exactly is the mechanism behind anxiety?

The Amygdala and Fight or Flight

If we look back hundreds of millions of years ago, before our brains developed the mechanism for anxiety, the only way animals could defend themselves from their environment was through preventative measures; they had thick skin, spines, or size to stop other animals from attacking them. The problem with these mechanisms was that eventually evolution caught up—animals evolved strong teeth to pierce thick skin and spines, and some formed groups to take down large prey.

For this reason, preventative measures were just not enough to guarantee survival. Living beings with a way to *react* to danger rather than prevent it would have a leg up. Thus, through random mutations and survival of the fittest, a reaction system began to develop—one that could help us quickly respond to danger in the moments right before it happened and that could not be outdone by evolution.

When this system first appeared hundreds of millions of years ago, the brain was not what it is today. Humans were not a distinct species yet, and those that did exist had very little brain power; they had the senses of sight, smell, and touch but no power to actually make meaning out of them—to think—the way we do now. This reactionary system needed to rely only on those senses and function without conscious thought.

The end result was an addition to the brain called the amygdala, two little clusters near the center. When the amygdala receives a stimulus from one of our senses, its job is to kick-start us into action so we can confront danger. In this way, the amygdala is like a simple computer program; it receives an input from our eyes, ears, or nose and outputs a performance-boosting hormone.

This idea is reflected in its structure. The amygdala is made of neurons (cells that carry electrical pulses) and synapses (the gaps between neurons). Together, these neurons and synapses connect to one another to make up networks, called synaptic pathways.

These synaptic pathways make up the amygdala's code; when the brain gets a message from our eyes or ears, it is translated into electrical signals and sent to the pathways in the amygdala, much like sending a password to a website.[3] If there are no pathways in the amygdala that say the stimulus is dangerous—if that password is not built into the code—the amygdala does not react. If it is, the amygdala starts a two-step chemical reaction throughout the body that helps it respond to that danger. First, it sends a message to the adrenal glands, located right above the kidneys. Then these glands produce adrenaline and release it into our bloodstream.[4]

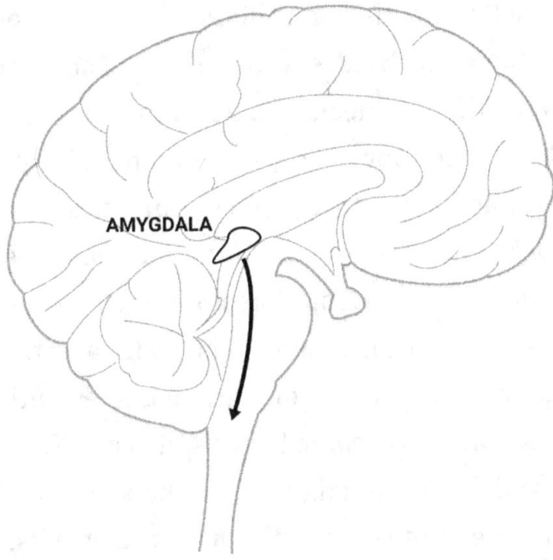

A diagram of the path from the amygdala to the adrenal glands.

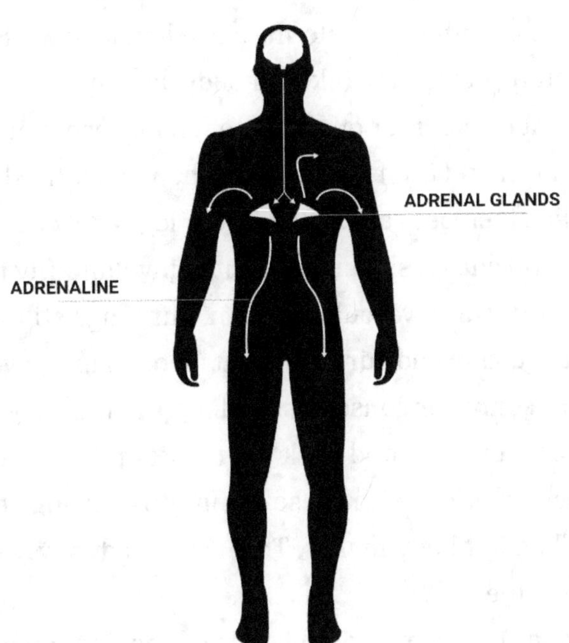

A diagram of adrenaline spreading from the adrenal glands through the blood.

This process, just like breathing and digestion, happens out of our conscious control. Our body decides what volume of adrenaline to make (usually way more than we need) and how much to send to each area of the body. This causes our heart to beat more quickly, our lungs to expand and contract more rapidly, and our muscles to become tense, all of which gives us an advantage in the face of danger; tense muscles make us stronger fighters, and rapid breathing makes us better runners. The technical term for this mechanism is the fight or flight response.

Since danger can come at a moment's notice, evolution drove the fight or flight response to become faster and faster. Today, the time it takes from amygdala to adrenaline is less than a tenth of a second.[3]

This system does not come without its drawbacks. Adrenaline puts a strain on our body due to how much energy it uses,[5] so it is only meant to be used in special circumstances and for a short time.

For this reason, rather than storing any adrenaline we do not decide to use for running or fighting (like our body does for certain other hormones), it is much safer for our body to forcibly use it outside of our conscious control and then make more whenever it needs to.

If adrenaline increases blood flow to our legs and we choose not to run, our legs still shake, shiver, and twitch involuntarily to release it. If it is sent to our cardiovascular system, our lungs still expand and contract more quickly and our heart beats more rapidly even if we are sitting down, resting, or consciously telling them to slow down. Our stomach turns, our arms and back get tense, and our eyes and ears become hypersensitive, with these symptoms getting stronger the more adrenaline our body makes. This is our body's way of using its leftover adrenaline.

This safeguard prevented our body from making too much adrenaline at once, but there is a second safeguard in our amygdala that prevents fight or flight from going on for too long: after a few minutes, our amygdala begins to calm its response and make less adrenaline, even if the sight or sound that set it off is still there.

Hundreds of millions of years ago, this response gave an advantage to those who had it. This helped living beings with an amygdala outlive those without one. This is why we see amygdalae in all mammals today—feline, canine, and of course primate (human).

Even though this system is millions of years old, our amygdala functions the same way today. We still receive boosts of adrenaline throughout our day, and any adrenaline we do not use gets used out of our control. While we sit at our desks or lie in bed, our leg muscles shake, our heart beats quickly, and our breath becomes shallow as a way for our body to put leftover adrenaline to use.

However, unlike our ancestors, our lives are no longer built around being able to run away whenever we feel like it. When we receive a shot of adrenaline in a business meeting or a class presentation, we have to let these sensations arise without being able to do anything with them. Thus we have come to see them as something negative—*unwanted* sensations produced by leftover adrenaline—which we named anxious symptoms.

We can see anxious symptoms in other mammals with amygdalae. For example, dogs run around and even shiver in the few minutes after they become excited. This helps them get rid of any adrenaline left in their body. The same is true for chimpanzees, deer, and even mice, who are known to shake, fidget, and show symptoms of involuntary adrenaline release shortly after getting scared.[6] However, the relationship humans and animals have with anxious symptoms is different for reasons we will discuss next.

The Emotional Brain and Suggestive Thoughts

Now that they had the amygdala, ancient mammals were prepared at the sight, smell, or sound of danger with an injection of fast-acting adrenaline. But as they began forming social groups, they could much more easily defend against other animals. In time, it was not other animals but rather ones in the same species that became the biggest risk—ones who all looked, smelled, and sounded the same—a threat that the amygdala was not complex enough to handle. And so, evolution trended toward those who could predict which of these were dangerous without needing to see, smell, or hear them.

To be able to predict danger rather than just respond to it, the brain had to develop new and physically separate sections. These could not replace the amygdala because immediate and unpredictable dangers would always be a problem, so they developed around and outside it. These new sections included the hippocampus and the hypothalamus, which are now collectively known as the limbic system. I will refer to the limbic system, not including the amygdala, as the **emotional brain**.

Our emotional brain evolved to dictate so many important unconscious functions, but for the purposes of this book, the most relevant one is the ability to bring things to our attention through basic thoughts.[7]

The most common thoughts our emotional brain creates are ones related to our senses. For example, when our stomach rumbles, the emotional brain produces a thought like *I may need to eat soon* and brings it to our attention. If we feel sleepy, it produces one like *I might want to sleep.*

It also creates thoughts about memories when we enter a situation we have been in before. For example, being in a situation where we experienced harm can cause our emotional brain to produce thoughts about danger, such as *Maybe I should get out of here.*[8]

Lastly, it can create thoughts of its own. We do not yet have an understanding of how this works, though we know our brain occasionally produces random and nonsensical thoughts, like *It might rain today* or *Maybe it would be bad to go outdoors.*

Together, these kinds of thoughts can be called suggestive thoughts, because they offer suggestions based on our senses, past experiences, and shots in the dark.

Suggestive thoughts gave ancient species a small advantage over one another; if they had a suggestive thought about being hungry, they could start hunting a little earlier. If they recalled a memory of a past danger, they could escape more quickly than others. And sometimes, even these shot-in-the-dark thoughts were correct.

However, the practical benefit of these thoughts is minor. The emotional brain can bring thoughts to our attention, but it cannot reason through them and decide which ones are actually helpful. Thus evolution trended toward those who could make this decision, causing yet another part of the brain to develop.

The Conscious Cortex and Worrying

With the evolution of great apes came the final and most important part of the brain: the prefrontal cortex.

Prior to the prefrontal cortex, our emotional brain was our command center. Whenever we received a cue from our body or our surroundings, we followed it—when our stomach rumbled and our emotional brain said *I should eat*, we ate. When we encountered an animal that brought up a negative memory, our emotional brain said *I should run*, and we ran.

In humans today, the emotional brain still handles reactionary behaviors in the first few seconds when we sense something new (which earned it the name fast brain). These include jumping out of our seat when we hear a loud noise or turning our head when we see something out of the corner of our eye. But the addition of the prefrontal cortex allows us to choose all of the actions after that—to ignore these knee-jerk behaviors and act differently (using our slow brain).[9]

When we think of who *we* are—the long-term decision maker of our life, the conscious being at the center of our body—it is in the prefrontal cortex. For this reason, throughout this book, I will refer to it as the **conscious cortex**.

Macroscopically, we have a good idea of how we make decisions in our conscious cortex. When a thought is produced in our emotional brain and brought to our attention in the conscious cortex, we analyze it—we determine whether we should act on it or ignore it. There are many theories as to how exactly this works, but all of them involve a basic **cost-benefit analysis**.[10]

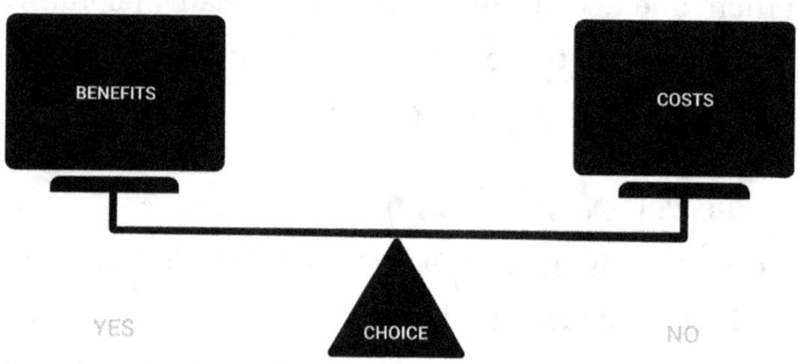

A visual of what a cost-benefit analysis looks like.

Practically, we start off by asking ourselves whether taking action would benefit us. We do so by making a short list of what we think we would gain and how much. Then, we ask if it would come at any sort of cost, like energy or time, and how much. These are called **valuations**, the factors we weigh and how much weight we give to each. After weighing our valuations, we make a decision and act on it. In other words, we act the way we do because we think we will gain something or because we think it will help us avoid losing something.

For example, every day our body produces hunger hormones and our emotional brain says *Maybe I should eat*. If we have nothing going on, we feel the benefit of not being hungry is high, while the time and energy costs are low. Thus we decide to eat and then physically act on that decision.

If we are hungry in an important business meeting, we might consider the cost of getting yelled at far larger than the benefit of not being hungry. In that case, the costs outweigh the benefits, so we choose not to eat and get back to what we were doing.

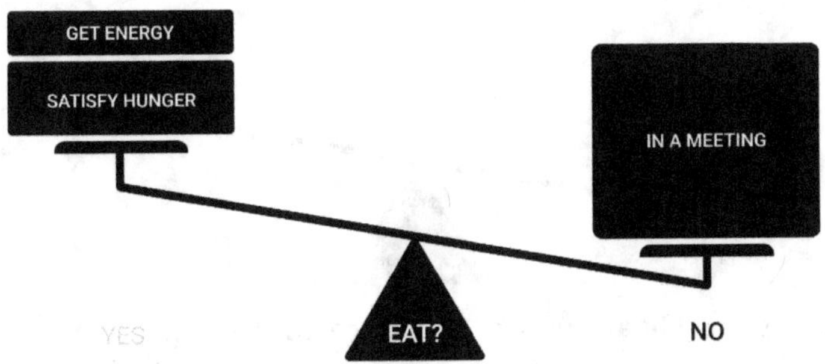

What our cost-benefit analysis might look like for the above scenario. The value of getting energy, satisfying hunger, and being in a meeting vary from person to person.

However, there is a third option, one that is not often discussed but is (ironically) the one we do the most: *consider* the thought further. If we think we cannot act immediately but we believe thinking more will help, we choose to continue considering the thought.

If we are hungry in the middle of a casual activity like doing homework or exercising, we might feel the costs of stopping outweigh the benefits. However, ignoring the thought does not solve our problem. Thus we choose to consider it further—to ask ourselves questions about when we should stop and what we should eat when we finish. After a while, when we feel the cost of being hungry outweighs the benefit of continuing our activity, we act on that thought and finally eat.

This brings to light an important distinction: in English, we define "behavior" as the choice to do something *physical*—to sleep or stay awake, to leave the house or stay at home, to eat or refrain. But that third option, to continue considering, is just as much of a calculated choice as the other two, meaning we do it because we think we will gain or lose something.

This is why, throughout this book, I will use the word **behavior** not only to refer to acting on or ignoring thoughts but also the action of considering them further.

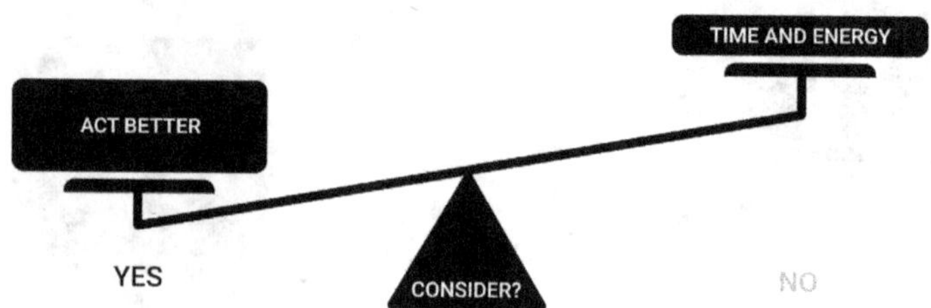

A generic cost-benefit analysis for our choice to further consider a suggestive thought rather than act on it or ignore it.

This is where worrying comes in. Worrying is a subset of the choice to consider a thought further; specifically, **worrying** is the choice to further consider a thought about something uncomfortable. When our emotional brain makes a suggestive thought about danger or discomfort, we can ignore it if we think the cost of doing something will outweigh any benefit, and we can physically act on it if we have a way to prepare. But most importantly in the context of this book, we can worry about it—ask ourselves questions about what that future danger might look like and play out scenarios in our head of all the different possibilities. This is the choice we make if we believe the benefit of worrying will outweigh the cost or if we believe the cost of *not* worrying will be high.

A generic cost-benefit analysis for our choice to worry.

As an example, after getting sick, our emotional brain might say *Is this more than a cold*? If we value our health highly, we may choose to further consider the thought rather than ignoring it. This might eventually lead us to make the doctor's appointment where we get diagnosed and treated. Or if we value financial security, we may respond to a suggestive thought like *Do I have enough money?* by further considering it. This may lead us to discover that our bank account is running low, and the worrying we choose to do after might help us make a budget.

A cost-benefit analysis for our choice to worry about illness.

Even if we are not aware of it, we cycle through these analyses every time a thought comes into our conscious cortex, and the way we behave is a result of this.[11] If we think of our emotional brain as a royal advisor offering us suggestions, our conscious cortex is the king—the one responsible for ultimately deciding what to do with them.

With such a difficult job, our conscious cortex cannot be a simple input-output system like the amygdala or the emotional brain—it needs to be able to respond to all thoughts it receives, regardless of how much code it has about them. Thus, while the general structure of the neurons and synapses in the conscious cortex is similar to the amygdala and the emotional brain, their function is different—like different programs being built in the same programming language. Our amygdala and emotional brain only accept certain inputs,[3] and the number of synaptic pathways (lines of code) decides how strong the output is.

The cortex is closer to an artificial intelligence (AI) program. In the conscious cortex, the number of synaptic pathways does not decide our response—it is built to consider all the thoughts from our emotional brain (regardless of how many synaptic pathways we have built around them) and decide what to do, much like an AI program accepts all inputs and makes educated-guess outputs.

In the conscious cortex, the number of pathways decides how easy it is to respond in a certain way—the more pathways we have for an action, the more comfortable, more efficient, or easier it becomes to respond in that way. Like the volume of leg muscles we have dictates how easily we can run or lift weight, the number of synaptic pathways we have for a certain action—like choosing to run, eat, sleep, or worry—decides how easily we can make that decision.[12]

This ability is what separates us from the rest of the animal kingdom—the reason why, despite our weak bodies, we are still at the top of the food chain. Our ability to weigh information and make decisions allowed our ancestors to outlive even the biggest and strongest animals.

It also means we are no longer at the whim of our hormones. Quite the contrary—the conscious cortex allows us to ignore our senses if we decide it will benefit us.

Now, if our stomach rumbles during a meeting and our emotional brain says *Maybe I should eat,* we can choose to ignore that thought. If we have an urgent problem while we are in class and encounter the thought *Maybe I should go take care of this,* we can choose to go despite all the consequences. And if we have a thought about future discomfort, like *Is eating this going to make me sick?*, we can choose to further consider it before we physically act.

The Cortex-Amygdala Interaction

The conscious cortex gave our ancestors a second weapon against danger. They had the amygdala's adrenaline release and the emotional brain for immediate dangers, and the slower conscious cortex to think ahead.

These two parts of the brain function this way today, but with one major nuance: they communicate with each other; if one part of our brain senses danger, it can prepare the other areas.

This happens in two ways. First, when our amygdala produces adrenaline and blood flows through our body more quickly, it energizes the emotional brain.[13] This causes it to produce suggestive thoughts more quickly and become faster to pull the trigger on reactionary behaviors like jumping out of our seats. But far more important than adrenaline's effect on our brain is our brain's effect on adrenaline.

Specifically, when we consider danger in the conscious cortex—*when we worry*—it signals to the amygdala that we will be in trouble soon, causing it to start producing adrenaline.[13]

This process looks almost exactly like the one you saw above. The difference here is what causes the amygdala to send that signal. In animals, the starting signal for adrenaline can only come from the amygdala. However, only in humans, *the signal can also come from the cortex.*[14]

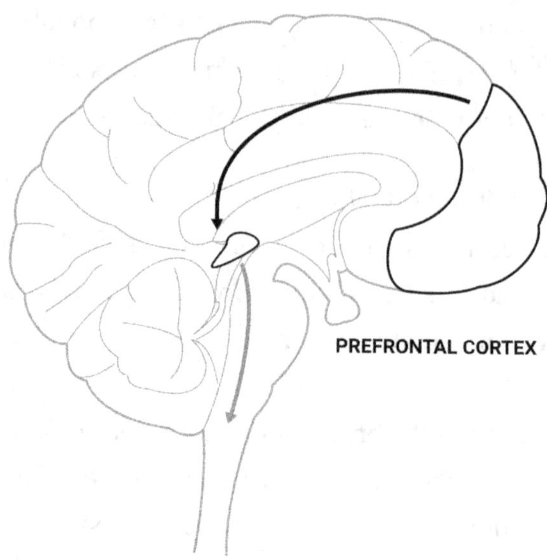

Diagram showing how worrying causes our brain to produce adrenaline. The cortex is linked to a structure within the extended amygdala, called the bed nucleus of the stria terminalis (BNST), which is what allows it to produce adrenaline.

This means that, when we worry, it produces enough adrenaline to raise our heart rate, tense our muscles, and even dilate our pupils.[15]

This brings to light one of the most important concepts in this book. Before our cortex formed, the things that caused our body to activate fight or flight and make adrenaline were only *external*, *visible*, and *tangible*, like smells, sights, and sounds. But now, with the cortex, there comes a new kind of stimulus: worrying.

Though, it is invisible and intangible, *worrying produces adrenaline*.

Just by considering thoughts about discomfort, we can induce a physical change in our body strong enough to cause all of the involuntary symptoms associated with adrenaline—from heart palpitations and nausea all the way to depersonalization. When we consider thoughts like *What if I fail my performance?* or *What if I say something embarrassing to my coworkers?*, it is our worrying, and *not* the amygdala's built in response, that causes us to experience anxious symptoms.

The Amygdala, the Emotional Brain, the Conscious Cortex, and Change

Evolution has left us all with amygdalae and cortexes with all of the functions discussed above. But our muscles and organs are not static, they can adapt; when we introduce our muscles to stress through exercise, our body reinforces them so we become stronger. When we go for a long time without stress, our body tears down these muscles to save energy and resources. If we introduce the muscles to too much stress at once, or not consistently, our body takes it as a freak event and does not change.

The brain works the same way. When we introduce our brain to constant stress over a long period of time, it builds the areas of the brain (the synaptic pathways) used to handle that stressor, and tears down the ones that do not. It is firm but shapeable, resistant to a strong and immediate force but receptive to a slow and gradual one.[16] The scientific term used to describe this phenomenon—the brain's ability to change itself—is neuroplasticity. Neuro- refers to our neurons, while plasticity means something capable of being molded or shaped. Neuroplasticity is something mistakenly attributed only to young people, but in truth, our brain is malleable for our entire lives.[17]

While the stress our muscles undergo is straightforward, it becomes a little more complex for our brain; since the amygdala, the emotional brain, and the conscious cortex all take different inputs, the only way we can apply stress to them is through these inputs.

The amygdala's inputs are our senses, so the way we apply stress is by overloading our senses—by overexposing ourselves to a sight, sound, or smell that causes our amygdala to activate. When we do this, our amygdala undergoes the same kind of buildup and breakdown that our muscles do; if this experience ends in harm or discomfort, the amygdala builds more synaptic pathways for that sight, sound, or smell. This means that, on our next encounter with it, the amygdala will be more sensitive, making more adrenaline in a shorter time. If the experience ends positively, the amygdala tears down those pathways, desensitizing it and causing it to make less adrenaline.[18]

There is some minor evidence that this process is influenced by genetics,[19] affecting how quickly and easily our brain becomes sensitive. But sensitivity can only be changed by experience.[20]

The emotional brain changes in a way similar to the amygdala—positive experiences cause it to dial up its production of suggestive thoughts and reactionary behavior, while negative experiences cause it to dial them down. Here, whether an experience is positive or negative is decided by our conscious reaction to it. If we react to a thought by choosing to act on it or considering it further, the emotional brain considers it positive and makes it more often. If we choose to ignore the thought, it is considered unhelpful, and the emotional brain produces it less often.[21]

The conscious cortex undergoes a different kind of change; when we choose to use a certain valuation, the conscious cortex builds synaptic pathways for us to do so again. When we choose to worry, the pathways not dedicated to worrying are torn down and then rebuilt to help us worry again—just like exercise does to our muscles. When we do not worry for a while, the brain tears down the synaptic pathways devoted to worrying.

This process of adopting and abandoning valuations starts as soon as we start to make conscious choices in our childhood. When we are young and our conscious cortex is not fully developed, we mimic the valuations of our parents and develop ones that help us stay safe at home.[22] For example, we know that children raised in abusive households become more comfortable valuing distrust, like of their parents, and experience more suggestive thoughts warning them away from trusting others as a way to protect them from parental abuse. Children who are harshly criticized by their parents become comfortable valuing self-blame because blaming themselves protects them from their parents' anger.[23]

However, once we reach young adulthood and our conscious cortex fully develops, we become able to expose ourselves to different valuations, even when they make us uncomfortable, or choose to abandon our current ones even when it takes a lot of effort. The more we expose ourselves to these different lines of thinking, the more comfortable we become thinking that way.

This means that just like our environment can impact our valuations when we are young, we become able to *change our own valuations* once we reach adolescence—to make our own brain build and break synaptic pathways so it becomes easier to make the choices we want.

This is the last key concept necessary to understand how anxiety disorders develop.

The Three Mechanisms

As you can see, what we have been calling anxiety—the symptoms we experience, the thoughts that pop into our head, and our mental behavior—is **not** actually one single mechanism. Yet in the English language, we group them all under one vague term, anxiety, rather than several separate ones.

This is why we have had so much trouble understanding it; when we look at anxiety as one cohesive mechanism, it becomes impossible to separate the symptoms from our behavior.

To properly understand anxiety, we have to abandon this definition and all the diagnoses that result from it (social anxiety, generalized anxiety, agoraphobia, obsessive compulsive disorder, etc). Instead, we must use different terms that make a distinction between the mechanisms you learned about in this chapter.

For this, there are a few distinct terms I will use throughout this book. First, I will use **anxious symptoms** to refer to the adrenaline-fueled symptoms that our amygdala produces out of our control. I will use **stress** and **stressors** to refer to any situation that our amygdala has become sensitive to (whether or not it is something we would typically consider stressful).

Next, I will use **suggestive thoughts** to refer to the thoughts our emotional brain creates, and **reactionary behaviors** to refer to the knee-jerk reactions our emotional brain has in the first few seconds of its response—both of which are out of our control.

And lastly, I will use **conscious worrying**, or simply worrying, to refer to the behavior we *do* control—to continue considering a thought rather than acting on or ignoring it—which we do in our conscious cortex.

How We Develop Anxiety Disorders

These separate systems—the conscious cortex, the anxious response from the amygdala the emotional brain, and the interaction between them—are present in everyone. This section is dedicated to understanding why some people worry excessively and experience much worse anxious symptoms.

Excessive, Irrational Worrying

The first problem we will cover is excessive worrying. As you read, we worry for the same reason as all our other behaviors: we think it will benefit us or that not doing it will come at a cost. More specifically, the benefit of worrying is that it helps us prepare for or prevent danger. The cost is the time and energy we put into it, as well as the mental discomfort of having to imagine an uncomfortable situation.

Just like any other kind of behavior, worrying can be productive. As shown earlier, worrying about money can lead us to check our bank account and budget for the month. Worrying about getting sick can lead us to make a doctor's appointment and get medicine to treat an illness. This kind of worrying is productive because our valuations are realistic—they lead us to worry at appropriate times, prevent us from worrying for too long, and help us take helpful physical actions.

When our valuations are healthy, we will not choose to worry when it takes too much time or energy.

However, worrying is not always productive—when we have been given incorrect information, worrying can be highly unproductive, even when our valuations are realistic and healthy. If our bank makes an error and makes us believe we are out of money, we may spend hours budgeting out the rest of our month, only to find out it was completely unnecessary. If we mistakenly read online that a physical symptom we have is a sign of serious illness, we may spend the whole week thinking about it or even drive to the ER, only to find out it was totally harmless.

We do not often worry because we are misinformed, so in the psychological community, worrying due to misinformation is not considered unhealthy. It is a kind of neutral behavior that is not productive but does not usually hold us back.

More often, we worry in unproductive ways because our valuations are unrealistic—we drastically over- or undervalue one of the factors in worrying, which causes us to keep doing it even when it is not productive anymore.

If we value not losing money so highly that we believe losing even a single cent is a major setback, we will choose to worry far more than is useful. If we value preventing an illness so highly that we do not even consider the costs, we will regularly sacrifice other areas of our life to ensure that we do not get sick.

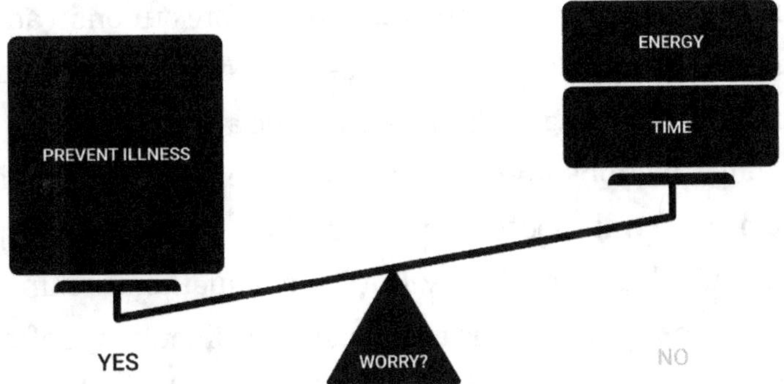

When our valuations are unhealthy, we will worry, even when it does not benefit us.

These are the kinds of valuations that cause us to worry in excessive, unhelpful, and illogical ways—the times when we waste energy worrying without getting any benefit and at the cost of time, energy, and discomfort.

The question is *how* our valuations manage to stray so far from reality. Now that you have read the previous section, the answer is clear: conditioning.[24]

Recalling from earlier, our brain shapes itself around the choices we make and the experiences we have. If we mimic our parents' unrealistic valuations or create our own when we are young, our brain will adjust—it will make it easier to keep thinking this way and harder to confront new valuations, even when our current line of thinking is unhealthy. Our emotional brain follows our behavior, making suggestive thoughts to support our conscious cortex, so we are reminded of these valuations more often. With enough time, our valuations can stray so far from reality that we choose to act in such excess that it hurts us. The technical name for this—a harmful behavior that we become so used to that we no longer think about it—is **cognitive blind spot**.

This is one of the many ways worrying is similar to eating. Eating appropriate amounts of food is necessary for us to survive. But if we value the pleasure we get from eating over our long-term health, we will choose to overeat. The more we do, the more our brain adjusts to continue overeating. Eventually, we become cognitively blind to our overeating, only noticing it when we are made aware by another person.

Worrying functions in the same way—when our valuations make logical sense, we will choose to worry only occasionally and stop when it takes too much time or energy. But if our valuations are unrealistic, we will worry excessively. This makes it more difficult to confront new valuations, and eventually we worry without realizing how much it hurts us.

In both cases, the benefit of acting gets smaller, and the smaller it is, the more excessively we do it. But the cost of challenging our valuations also increases. At some point, our actions become less about acting for benefit and more about preventing the cost that comes with thinking differently: the energy it would take for our brain to change. This is how our brain *gradually* becomes geared toward excessively worrying—healthy behaviors *become* unhealthy when we do them to avoid feeling uncomfortable rather than to benefit us.

If you have heard the term "natural worrier," this is what it means; the valuations we use have caused our brain to be comfortable with worrying. This comfort does not mean we are forced to worry—we can always change our valuations so that we choose to act differently. But as opposed to those whose brains have not been built up in this way, natural worriers have the *added cost* of experiencing mental discomfort when choosing not to worry.

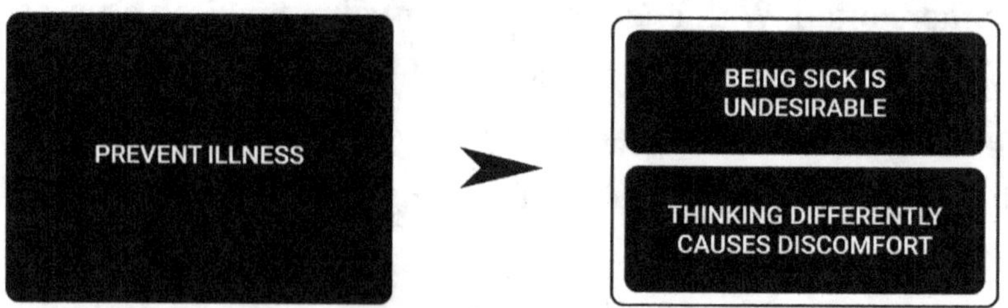

The more we choose to think in a certain way, the more uncomfortable it becomes to think differently.

This conditioning is how we grow into patterns of excessive worrying. However, if this was the full story behind anxiety disorders, we would have found the solution long ago.

Panic

The next piece of the puzzle is the amygdala. When our amygdala encounters a stressor, it tells our body to produce adrenaline, which gets sent to our muscles and organs. This gives them a boost in energy and causes all of the anxious symptoms associated with adrenaline. There are certain safeguards in place to prevent fight or flight from lasting too long or being too strong: the amygdala dials down its response over time, and our body releases as much adrenaline as it needs to.

However, the cue to create adrenaline can come from one other place: the conscious cortex. When we consciously worry, this has just as much power to create adrenaline as the amygdala does on its own—to lead our throat muscles to tense up, our knees to get shaky, or our stomach to churn outside of our conscious control.

All the worrying we do in the conscious cortex results in symptoms, but the strength of these is usually limited. It is normal for those who frequently worry about their job—surgeons, investment bankers, politicians—to experience mild anxious symptoms like an elevated heart rate, nausea, and trouble sleeping more often than those with less demanding jobs.[25]

However, in a select group of people, our body keeps making adrenaline, far beyond what is appropriate for the situation; instead of a heart rate that briefly spikes up and slows down, some of us have a heart rate that keeps escalating, often to 150+ bpm for a half hour or more. Rather than our nausea intensifying for a minute at the beginning of a meeting then fading away, it continues to build, causing us to dry heave and even vomit.[26] These anxious symptoms can get so strong they cause many of us to drop what we are doing and call an ambulance.

This cannot be caused by the amygdala alone—it can only sustain fight or flight for a few minutes. It also cannot be caused by just any worrying, otherwise every surgeon and banker would be constantly jittery and nauseated.

Instead, a certain number of us experience this giant boost of adrenaline in average situations, like at our desk at work or in class. We are speaking to a coworker or taking notes in a meeting when we suddenly begin to get short of breath. Then in under a minute, our heart rate skyrockets, adrenaline shoots through our body, and we feel the overwhelming urge to escape—we experience **panic**—independent of what is happening around us.

Panic includes all of the mechanisms we have learned up until now, but in a specific way:

A panic attack occurs when we worry about *the symptoms of our worrying, forming a kind of loop.*

This may sound complex, but it becomes easy to understand when we break it down. When we worry, it causes our body to create adrenaline, leading to rapid breathing, tense muscles, and nausea. If we worry *about* these symptoms, it (paradoxically) sends a response to the amygdala to release *more* adrenaline, which causes these symptoms to get stronger.

In practice, it functions like this.

1. We experience a symptom like an elevated heart rate. It can come as a result of some other behavior like exercise, because we were worrying about something unrelated, or because we got poor sleep or were dehydrated.

2. Our emotional brain creates a suggestive thought about that symptom, like *Is this dangerous?* and becomes jumpy.

3. We briefly weigh the benefits of worrying about this thought (something like preventing a possible heart attack) against the costs. If we think it will benefit us, we worry—we ask ourselves questions about whether our heart is about to fail and whether we need to call an ambulance.

4. This worrying signals to the amygdala that it is in danger, causing it to produce adrenaline. This brings us back to step 1 but with stronger symptoms.

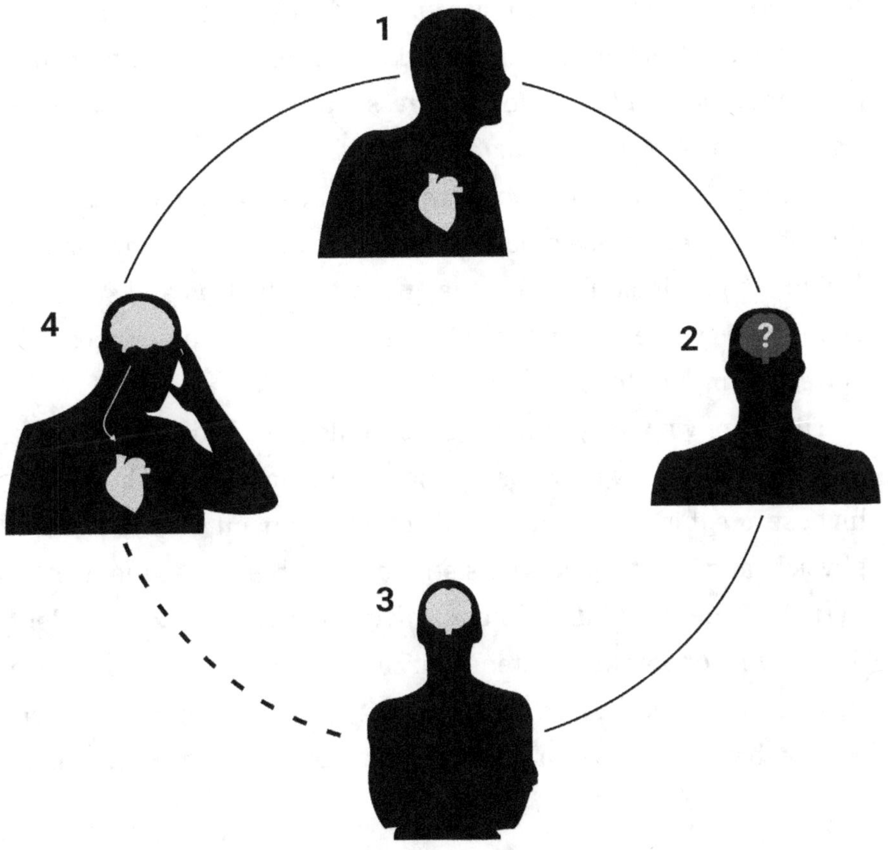

The four steps of the panic spiral.

If the initial symptom and suggestive thought are the spark, worrying is like fanning the flames. This new adrenaline causes our heartbeat to get faster and stronger (causing a more pronounced step 1). If we worry about it again (step 3), that leads the amygdala to produce even more adrenaline.

The cycle continues a few times, and our body makes so much adrenaline that it has to let it out through other sensations. In the first few seconds of this process, our adrenaline level is low enough that these sensations are minor, usually just a more energetic emotional brain—one that is jumpier and produces suggestive thoughts more frequently (step 2). These new thoughts may come with a sense of urgency like *Am I about to embarrass myself?* or *Do I need to leave right now?* or *Am I going crazy?*

If we continue to worry about the original symptom or these new thoughts, our amygdala produces even more adrenaline, until organs outside the brain start to feel the effect, like the legs and stomach. This causes some mild physical symptoms, like shaky knees and butterflies in the stomach.

The more we worry, the more adrenaline our body will produce. Eventually, our body hits a peak where it produces adrenaline at the highest rate it is physically capable of. At this point, we are hit with physical and mental symptoms strong enough to cause many of us to rush to the hospital: full-body shivers, extra heartbeats, violent dry heaving or vomiting, intense dizziness, and a flurry of intrusive thoughts about going crazy or dying. For most of us, the first experience with panic opens up a world of discomfort we never knew existed.

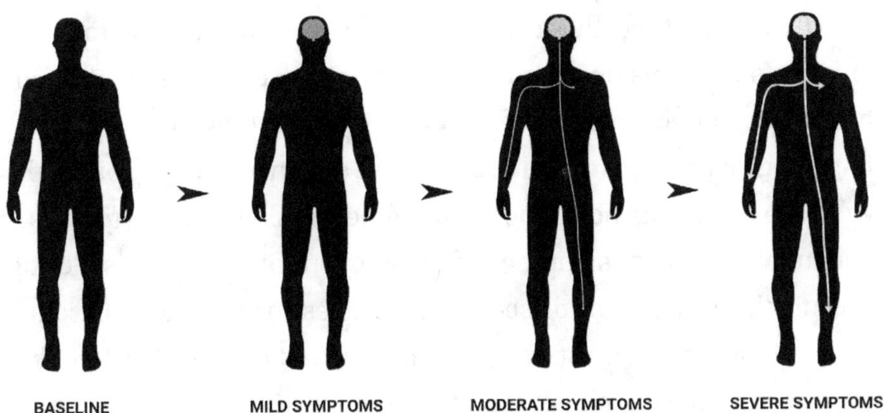

The progression of adrenaline and the anxious symptoms it causes during an episode of panic.

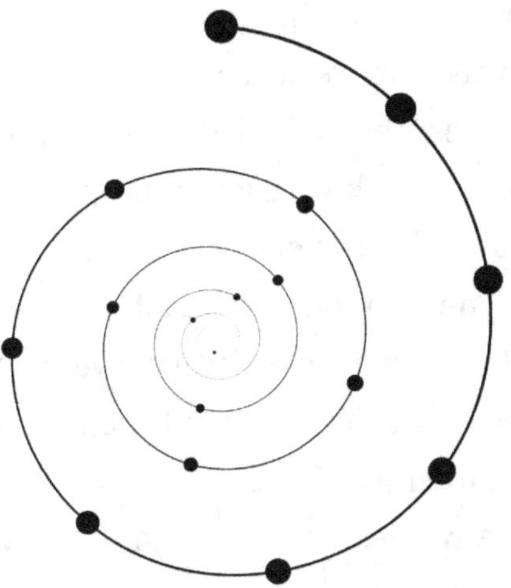

The panic spiral. Each time we worry, our symptoms get worse.

Everyone I know, myself included, clearly remembers their first panic attack. It is not an easy thing to forget. This first one typically lasts only a few minutes—if we have not conditioned our body to make a ton of adrenaline, it will eventually run out of steam.[27] But if we continue to worry about anxious symptoms every time they come up, our brain and body change to accommodate.

With enough time, they can regularly make enough adrenaline that anxious symptoms become a constant presence: nausea and rapid heartbeat multiple times a week, random intrusive thoughts constantly imposing on us for months at a time. If we continue to worry, our body will keep increasing how much adrenaline it makes, leading to worse and more consistent symptoms: frequent vomiting, daily episodes of irregular heartbeats, and dissociation that goes on indefinitely. In some of the worst cases, almost every waking moment can be filled with the strongest possible anxious symptoms, preventing us from regularly sleeping, eating, and even drinking. When I said I went from normal college student to someone who could barely function, this is why.

In the initial days I fell into the spiral, I had so many uncomfortable symptoms that it was hard to focus on just one. I was nauseated, but my worrying about it caused me to dry heave every time I tried to eat or drink. I got massive adrenaline rushes multiple times a day, but since I kept thinking about all of the negative things they could lead to, my body turned each one into full-body shakes that would sometimes last for hours. I got strong flashes of intrusive thoughts every couple of minutes, but because I worried about them every time they came, they kept coming harder and faster.

To make matters worse, the medication that was supposed to be helping me was not working, nor were the so-called anxiety-stopping techniques I was given, shattering any hope I had of getting better and giving me one more reason to worry. And as is unfortunately familiar to so many of us, every time I got in bed and began to drift off, my body jerked awake, ensuring I got no more than an hour of fractured sleep and making the next day even worse.

Avoidance and Phobias

After suffering through several episodes of panic in a certain situation, many of us begin to avoid it. This gives us temporary relief, but this avoidance comes at a cost: when we avoid a situation we have panicked in, our behavior reinforces to the amygdala that the situation is negative, even when it logically is not. This causes our amygdala to build more synaptic pathways around this behavior, causing it to produce more adrenaline on our next encounter.[28] This can also function like a spiral: we experience anxious symptoms somewhere, like at a store or in our car. We worry about the discomfort this could cause, leading us to leave the situation. This makes our amygdala become more sensitive to it. The next time we enter this situation, we will experience even stronger symptoms, which, if we are still thinking in the same way, will make us even less likely to stay.

After tens or hundreds or thousands of avoidances, the volume of adrenaline our amygdala produces can cause us to hit levels we see in panic, leading to full-body shakes, high heart rate, nausea, and vomiting. But through avoidance, these symptoms become specific to the situation.[28] This kind of conditioning is what we know as a phobia.

We are most likely to have panic attacks, and thus most likely to develop phobias, in situations that most of us worry about and want to avoid—vulnerable social situations like public speaking or tense physical situations like flying in a plane.[29] But there are so many factors besides external stress that can cause panic-like symptoms.

Our heart rate could start elevating because we are about to step on stage for a performance, because we just walked up a flight of stairs, or because we did not get enough sleep the night before. If we worry about these symptoms, we are capable of having a panic attack and thus developing a phobia in any situation. As proof of this, the medical world has recorded and given names to hundreds of different kinds of phobias, from the more common ones like social phobia to outlandish ones we see on reality TV.

Compulsions

Another way we can condition ourselves is by developing compulsions—harmful, unproductive, or bizarre behaviors we feel the need to keep repeating at risk of experiencing uncomfortable thoughts or symptoms. Though they may look different from phobias on the outside, the cause is the same: conditioning. That is, when we act a certain way over and over again, our brain will build around continuing to act that way, even if it hurts us.[30]

These behaviors usually start logically, giving us some benefit and coming at a minor cost. For example, some actions like biting our nails and pulling at our hair help us release pent up adrenaline, even when we do not realize it. In fact, when we do these infrequently, they are not considered compulsions at all. But if we bite and pull so often we feel uncomfortable without them, we may have to resort to more and more intense behavior just to be comfortable—biting our fingernails until we bleed or pulling our hair so hard it comes out in clumps.

Other behaviors are tied to worrying, which can also be logical at first. Worrying about impacting others may lead us to check our emails and messages before we send them. If we do this so often we feel uncomfortable without it, we may end up reading and rereading our emails over twenty times—something I did throughout university.

Worrying about health, as described earlier, can lead us to take certain actions to help us make sure we are not sick. If we feel uncomfortable without worrying, we might google our symptoms without ever going to a doctor—a habit I had for decades. We might also think to wash our hands more frequently to avoid ingesting germs. However, as we grow more comfortable behaving in these ways, we may find ourselves doing them more and more often, to the point where they cause us physical harm—spending so much time googling that we lose sleep or washing our hands so often and for so long that it wears down our skin.

Occasionally, we see compulsions whose origins are hard to determine—behaviors that do not seem like they could ever provide us benefit, like counting to specific numbers, repeating behaviors a certain number of times, or behaving in ways that are overly superstitious. The way these develop is not yet fully understood, but I believe they are the result of a young mind that is not fully developed finding solutions that an adult brain might not consider.

For example, we might hear the old adage about stepping on a crack in the street when we are children, leading us to avoid stepping on cracks. Most children grow out of this phase, but if we are taught to overvalue superstition, we may continue to act in this way into adulthood. With enough repetition, our brain builds around it. After a while, we feel so uncomfortable without stepping on cracks that we get hit with strong suggestive thoughts and physical symptoms when we try to stop. Though we may lose that original memory of the adage, our comfort around this behavior—and the discomfort without it—stays with us.

Since many of us worry when we do not act on a compulsive urge, it is not uncommon for those of us who have compulsions to experience strong anxious symptoms when we behave differently.[31] This gives us even more incentive to continue acting on these urges.

The reason obsessive compulsions have been so difficult to understand is that the medical community has not had many chances to witness this gradual change. By the time doctors finally intervene, all they see is our behavior at that moment, not the decades of conditioning that led us to that point, nor the massive volume of adrenaline that is going through our system.

The Science of Recovery

When we look at anxiety in the traditional way, as one mechanism and in terms of chemical imbalances or disorders that we have to adjust, it is impossible to make sense of it. We gradually become more and more victimized by a genetic problem that we have not yet identified and can only find relief through medication (which itself is being called into question) and anxiety management techniques.[32]

However, when we split anxiety up into amygdala, cortex, and interaction, we see it is not a genetic disorder at all, like we had previously believed. Instead, the anxious symptoms and comfort around excessive worrying are our body's way of adapting to our behavior, the way it is supposed to.

When we look at worrying as a choice, rather than a complex imbalance of chemicals, we can understand it like all the other choices we make—as something we do because we think it will benefit us or because choosing not to would make us uncomfortable.

When we combine this idea with what we know about neuroplasticity, we can understand how we work ourselves into unhealthy amounts of worrying, just like we adjust to unhealthy amounts of eating and unhealthy levels of physical activity.

When we understand how worrying activates the amygdala, the connection between behavior and symptoms becomes clear. Just like maintaining bad posture causes pain, we can see how excessive worrying causes uncomfortable anxious symptoms.

And when we understand this connection is a behavioral feature and not a genetic fault, it finally makes sense why anyone can worry excessively, have panic attacks, and develop compulsions, regardless of their genetics.[33]

Within this new understanding comes a groundbreaking thought, one that unlocks infinite potential for treatment: if excessive worrying and anxious symptoms happen due to conditioning, then just like any other conditioning our body undergoes, it can be undone.

When we have been overeating for our entire lives, we may reach a point where we are constantly suffering from weight-related problems, like joint issues or liver dysfunction. By this point, challenging the values that make us overeat will feel uncomfortable. However, if we recognize the discomfort will only be temporary, and give value to our long-term health, we are able to choose differently—to eat healthily. Once we start eating less, our brain adjusts, making it mentally easier to do so again. After a few weeks, our body also adjusts by slowly reducing its production of hunger hormones and burning the fat. The end result is that, once our body reaches a normal weight and our diet is healthy, our weight-related problems go away.[34]

Conscious worrying and anxious symptoms work the same way. Our valuations may become so unrealistic they lead us to worry all the time, which will lead to constant anxious symptoms and an overactive emotional brain. But if we understand why this happens and how to change it, we become able to choose differently—to reexamine our valuations so that we choose not to worry, even if it feels temporarily uncomfortable. Over time, this leads our brain to become more comfortable without worrying, making it easier to worry less. As a result, the body will produce less adrenaline, slowly tuning down the strength and duration of anxious symptoms.

The less we worry, the more the brain and body do what they were built to do: readjust. The brain becomes more and more comfortable without worrying, and the adrenaline becomes less and less present.

In time, this means that we can do more than just manage anxious symptoms or cope with them, it means *we can return to baseline*—a baseline where we no longer worry excessively or regularly experience anxious symptoms.

The Process of Change

Inducing this change will take a lot of time and energy. The brain has almost a hundred billion neurons and over a hundred times more synapses, and we can only tear down so many at once.[16] To make them change, we have to put our brain under uncomfortable stress by exposing it to valuations it is not used to.

This will initially cause the equivalent of muscle fatigue in the brain, also known as **cognitive dissonance**. We will feel tired after challenging our valuations. Our emotional brain will send suggestive thoughts trying to stop us from changing. Anxious symptoms will come, even when we would be better off without them.

But this discomfort will be temporary. As we practice, our brain will reshape to make this exposure less uncomfortable, and it will become more comfortable with our new behavior. This will lead to fewer uncomfortable suggestive thoughts and symptoms as a result. In time, that new behavior will become second nature, and symptoms will fade away.

This means that no matter where we start from—mild symptoms or severe symptoms, social phobia or agoraphobia, occasional worrying or constant worrying—we can gradually push our brain back to a healthy baseline. In time, even the strongest compulsive urges will fade away, panic will no longer happen, and worrying will not be a major factor in our life.

Following this path will mean changing our understanding of mental health treatment. Currently, most therapies focus on management and coping. In other words, trying to live with the uncomfortable symptoms of our worrying and avoidance. But much like losing weight requires us to change our diet rather than just cope with the consequences of overeating, our approach to anxious symptoms must *focus on changing our mental behavior.*

Once we are comfortable eating less and drop to a healthy weight—once we are comfortable not worrying and physical symptoms are no longer a presence in our life—we can play around with coping and management techniques to deal with small problems. But our behavior, and not these management techniques, will always be the focus.

For this, I will introduce you to three therapies that will help you change your mental behavior.

Introduction to Treatment: MBCT, CBT, and ERP

In this book, we will cover three different therapies, each for a different mechanism in the brain: one for treating amygdala-cortex panic, one for treating excessive worrying in the conscious cortex, and one for desensitizing our amygdala's built-in fight or flight response.

In each section, I will give a brief explanation of the theory behind the therapy. Then I will explain how to apply it in a general setting. After that, I will give examples of how we can apply it in more specific settings, to give you ideas for how to do so yourself.

The first and most important therapy I will discuss in this book is mindfulness-based cognitive therapy (MBCT), which targets the amygdala-cortex interaction. This therapy will be most important for those who experience anxious symptoms, panic, and compulsive urges.

In the previous section, we saw that panic happens when we worry about anxious symptoms—our body produces a symptom, then our emotional brain makes a suggestive thought about it, we choose to worry, and that causes the symptom to become stronger, leading to a spiral. MBCT helps us cut out that third step—to quickly change our response to suggestive thoughts about our health so we choose not to worry, cutting off the body's ability to make more adrenaline.

When we practice it correctly, the initial symptoms will show up (especially at first), but rather than getting stronger and turning into panic, they will stay at the same level then slowly fade away. After a few weeks of MBCT, the body will produce less adrenaline, causing anxious symptoms to appear less often. After a few months, the symptoms will go away entirely.

MBCT is the backbone for the other two therapies but is especially important for the following:

- Panic attacks
- Uncomfortable physical symptoms, from sweating or butterflies in the stomach to more severe ones like nausea and vomiting or muscle tremors
- Uncomfortable mental symptoms like depersonalization, thoughts of going crazy, thoughts that are violent or bizarre, and compulsive urges

The second form of therapy we will cover is called cognitive behavioral therapy (CBT). Like MBCT, this therapy was designed to help us answer suggestive thoughts, but rather than being used for questions that are only about our short-term health, CBT is better for longer-term questions—about relationships, family, or work, to name a few—that need more time and effort to answer.

CBT works by looking at worrying, just like we did above, as a choice we make based on our valuations. CBT helps us piece apart our valuations, so we can see exactly where we were unrealistic, and choose to adopt new ones.

In the long term, commitment to CBT helps us cut out behavior based on unhealthy valuations, like excessive worrying. As a byproduct, this also leads our body to produce less adrenaline.

CBT is used to address the following:

- Worrying about a single subject for more than a few weeks
- Worrying before, during, or after social situations

- Worrying about the way others see us, resulting in low self-esteem
- Difficulty responding to negative emotions, like jealousy and anger

Where MBCT and CBT focus on the cortex, the last therapy, exposure and response prevention (ERP), targets the extended amygdala alone.

The amygdala's response is based on experience; experiences that end negatively make it more sensitive, and those that end positively make it less sensitive. ERP is our way to manually induce positive experiences for our amygdala so that it desensitizes.

For most, the biggest factor behind whether experiences end positively or negatively is the presence of panic—no matter how often we expose ourselves to a stressor, our amygdala will still count the experience as negative if we panic. For this reason, ERP is only effective when we couple it with a therapy that prevents us from falling into the panic spiral, like MBCT, to ensure every exposure ends positively.

ERP is used to reduce the intensity of symptoms which arise in the following situations:

- Social situations like public speaking or going to the gym
- With certain sensations, like taking off in a plane or elevator doors closing
- With compulsions like locking and unlocking doors or excessively rereading messages or emails
- In the presence of certain thoughts or memories

Since the way we worry and the symptoms we experience vary so much from person to person, each person's treatment plan will be different; there is no one-size-fits-all therapy, so finding the combination of therapies that works best for us will take a lot of exploring and experimenting.

For this reason, I organized the therapies in order of urgency and simplicity. The first therapy, MBCT, targets short-term panic using quick and easy answers. The second therapy, CBT, borrows techniques from MBCT to address long-term worrying. The last therapy, ERP, helps reduce the strength of anxious symptoms, but only once we have a handle on MBCT and CBT.

To find what overall method will work best for you, I recommend using just MBCT for at least two or three weeks until you get the hang of it. Then, add CBT for another two or three to see what combination of the two gives you the best results. Once you are used to practicing both, you can round out your treatment with ERP. This approach will help you quickly find the strategy that suits you best, without giving you too much to focus on at any one time.

Now, let us start with mindfulness-based cognitive therapy for panic and anxious symptoms.

MINDFULNESS-BASED COGNITIVE THERAPY

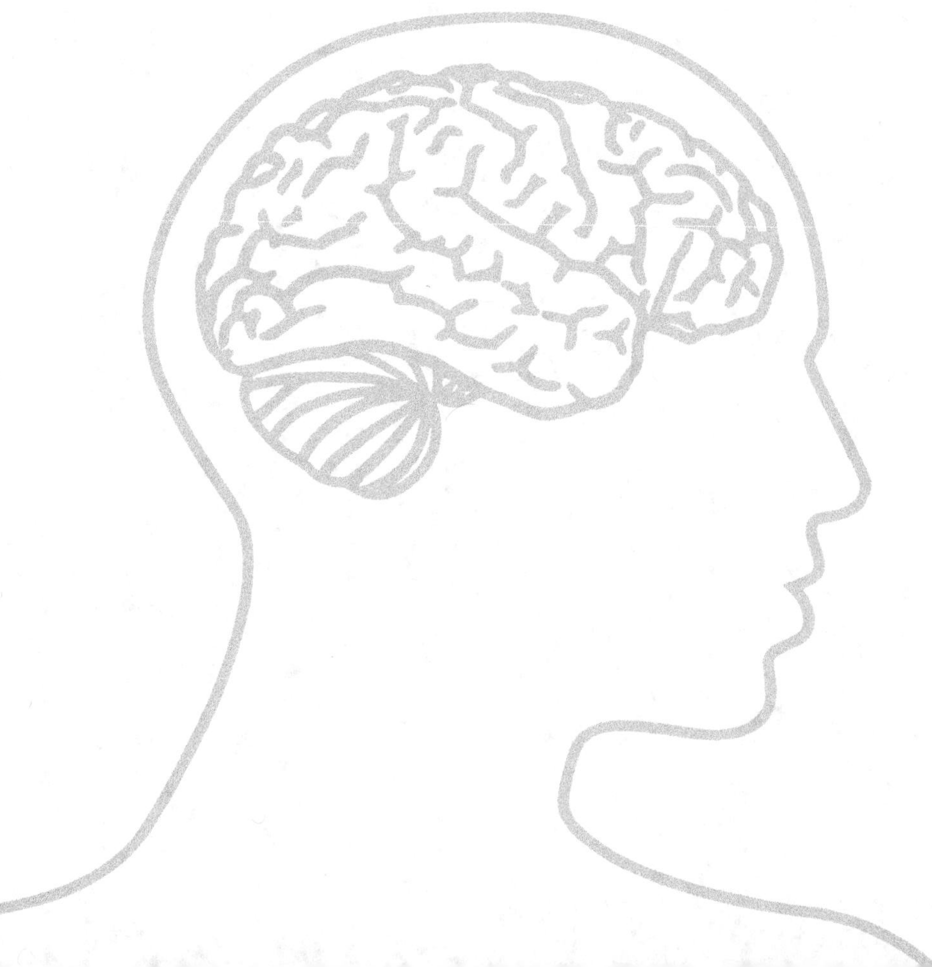

The MBCT Method for Anxious Symptoms and Panic

Mindfulness-based cognitive therapy will be our weapon against panic and high adrenaline. I start this chapter with a general introduction to MBCT methods, then go into how to apply them to the most common anxious symptoms, and finish with some general advice.

Throughout our lives, we will encounter many different symptoms and situations, so we will have to apply MBCT in different ways. For this reason, rather than giving you a premade set of responses, I will help you make your own.

The best way to read through this chapter is first to read about the theory and the method, then one or two symptoms you have trouble with, then the general advice section at the end of the chapter for some helpful tips.

Theory: The Panic Spiral

Recalling from a few chapters ago, panic happens when we worry about anxious symptoms. The process looks like the following:

1. We experience an anxious symptom out of our control.
2. Our emotional brain creates a suggestive thought about our health, also out of our control.
3. We choose to worry about it, sending the signal to the amygdala to get ready for danger.

4. The amygdala produces adrenaline out of our control, leading the symptoms to get stronger, and bringing us back to step 1.

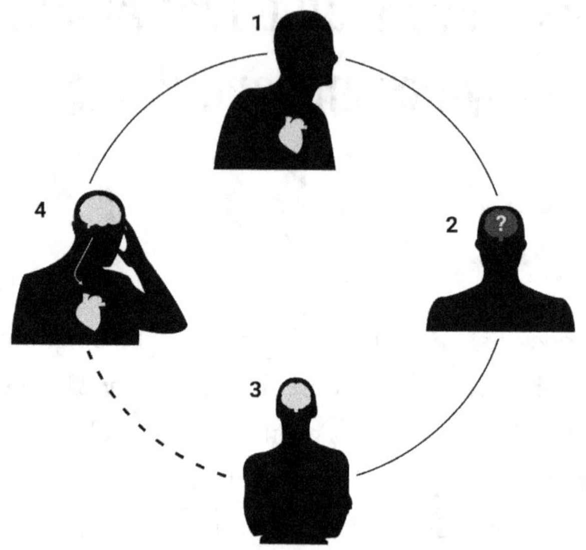

The four steps of panic.

PANIC WITHOUT INTERVENTION

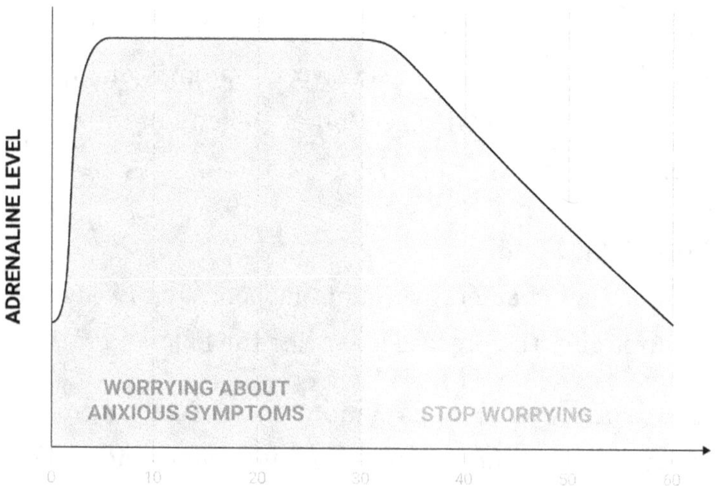

The timeline of panic without intervention.

In old treatment methods that did not recognize this pattern, people were often given so-called anxiety-stopping exercises, like breathing techniques. These techniques were meant to try to suppress that fourth step—the adrenaline release throughout our body—as slower breathing might cause a slight reduction in mild symptoms. This led some people who worried about those particular symptoms to experience minor relief.

However, no matter how hard we consciously try, *that fourth step will always be out of our direct control*; we can breathe as deeply as we want, but we cannot do anything to stop the wave of adrenaline the amygdala produces. In fact, rather than actually stopping adrenaline, these techniques only *redirect* symptoms to other areas of the body, like the muscles, causing them to jitter and shake more.

For this reason, such stopping techniques have been compared to scratching at a rash—our body is already releasing adrenaline and breathing on its own, and trying to get in its way is not only unnecessary but also leads us to worry (and produce more symptoms) when we fail. For this reason, author Barry McDonagh[35] says relying on these stopping techniques is a lot like jumping into quicksand: the more we fight to break free of anxious symptoms, the more they suck us in.

Instead of focusing our efforts on a step of the process we cannot control, we should focus on the one we can: step three—our worrying.

When we change our behavior, we break free of the cycle after just a few spins; our amygdala will produce adrenaline and our emotional brain will suggest thoughts, but rather than getting worse because we worry, they will level out and slowly go away.

In other words, the key to ending panic is *experiencing anxious symptoms without worrying about them*. When we do so, we stop the spiral dead in its tracks and let the body release adrenaline without making more.

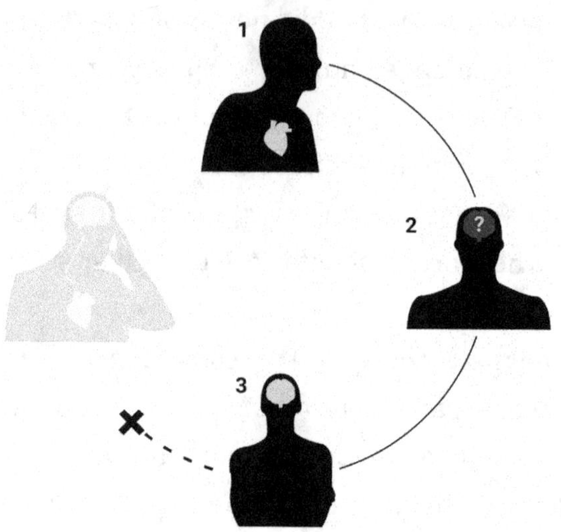

How to stop panic: remove the third step.

When done correctly, the first few waves of adrenaline will come, but the symptoms will not get worse, as they do in panic. Rather, we will experience them for a minute or two, then they will slowly turn into milder symptoms until our body releases all of the leftover adrenaline.

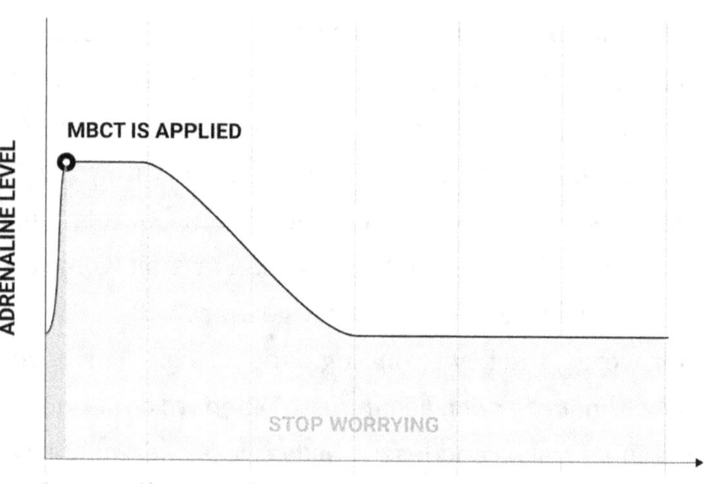

The timeline of panic with intervention.

Mindfulness-based cognitive therapy is the way of applying this idea. The MBCT method in this chapter will help us quickly minimize the benefits and maximize the costs of worrying in our head. That way, when a suggestive thought arises, we choose not to worry about it, leading our body to stop producing more adrenaline.

The MBCT method consists of four steps: **recognize**, **respond**, **return**, and **remind**.

MBCT Method: Recognize

The cue to start the MBCT process is *when a suggestive thought about an anxious symptom enters our head.* Our first step: recognize that thought.

By recognizing, I mean spelling out the *exact* thought we are worrying about. This might seem obvious to some, especially those of us who have practiced doing so in therapy or meditation. But if we have been worrying for most of our lives, it almost feels like we are worrying about nothing.

The simplest way we can practice recognition is by answering the question "What am I worrying about?" Our answer should be simple but specific—a few clear words. For example, *I am worrying I won't be able to catch my breath, I am worrying I am having a heart attack,* or *I am worrying that I am going crazy.* The shorter and more specific our answer, the easier the following steps will be.

This step is the key to the rest of the process because we have to know what thought we are trying to address before we apply techniques to it. Many people I have worked with are so eager to jump into the other steps that they forget this one and end up stuck, so make sure to give it proper attention.

This concludes the first step: **R**ecognize the thought we are worrying about.

MBCT Method: Respond

Once we have found the thought we are worrying about, the next step is to respond to it in a way that helps us choose not to worry. To do this, we have to minimize the benefits of worrying and raise the costs—to help us understand why we do not need to worry.

To help us in this step, I would like you to examine your history with anxious symptoms. Despite all the panic you have experienced, you are still here. You have not had a heart attack, stopped breathing, or gone crazy like your emotional brain has suggested, even though each time, it said this would be *the* panic attack that ruins everything.

You are still alive, and you are still sane. In fact, you have probably already been through some of the scariest experiences your emotional brain has brought up—embarrassment, illness, physical danger, heartache—and made it through just the same.

The backbone of all MBCT methods, the idea that underlies the entire recovery process, is gathered from our own experience—*anxious symptoms are harmless, so we do not need to worry about them.* In fact, worrying about anxious symptoms has gotten us nowhere and has not actually protected us from danger. So as comfortable as we might be worrying about these symptoms, the cost has been enormous—hundreds or thousands of hours of anxious discomfort.

The response portion of MBCT is how we apply this idea. Once we have recognized the suggestive thought that is troubling us, we say a few quick words to immediately shut down any desire to worry about it. This can take many forms, but a generic response that works for many people is saying, *Okay, whatever, I know it'll be fine.* As our heart starts to beat more quickly and we identify a thought about our chest exploding, we say to ourselves, *Okay, whatever, so let it happen. My heart has done this a thousand times before. I know this symptom will go away as quickly as it came.*

This applies to any thought our emotional brain makes:

What if I am wrong and my heart really is about to fail? Okay, whatever, someone nearby will see me and help.

What if I stop watching my breathing and I pass out? Okay, whatever, let it happen already. I would rather stop breathing than keep worrying forever.

What if this is a sign that I am actually going crazy? Okay, whatever, it is out of my control anyway, so I guess I'll go crazy.

This is just *one* example of a response we can give. I have heard responses that are compassionate (*You'll be alright, I promise*), sarcastic (*Oh, here come those big scary symptoms again. Look out everyone, my heart rate is slightly faster*). I have heard clinical (*These are just symptoms my body is using to release adrenaline. As long as I let them come and go without worrying about them, my body will return to baseline on its own*) and detached (*Ah, screw it, I don't care. Let it happen*). Different people and different situations require different answers, so play around with your answer to find out which one works best in the moment.

When we do this correctly, our symptoms will still be there, but rather than feeling like a threat, they will feel like a small annoyance we can work through, like a headache or an upset stomach—symptoms we know will go away soon but that we can deal with for a little bit. The end goal is to get comfortable experiencing all these uncomfortable symptoms. As long as we do that, our body will stop producing more adrenaline.

In summary, the second step of the MBCT process is this: **R**espond to our most pressing thought.

MBCT Method: Return

Once we have answered the suggestive thought, we must avoid checking whether the original symptom has gone away because checking is another form of worrying. If we truly understand our symptoms are harmless and temporary, we have no need to check for them. But if we continue to consider the thought *Shouldn't I worry about that?*, the answer will eventually feel like it should be yes even when we know it is not. As the expression goes, "If we keep looking for problems, we will find them," even when they are not there.

To prevent ourselves from self-checking, the best thing we can do is focus on something that grabs our attention—to *return* our focus to an activity that keeps us occupied and shuts down the urge to check in.

If we are in the middle of an activity, this will mean focusing on the last thing we did—if we are speaking to someone, we can ask ourselves, *What did they just say?* If we are in class, we might recall the last thing our professor said.

If we are not in the middle of anything, returning means occupying ourselves with something. The best activities are ones that require us to be creative or analytical, like drawing and playing an instrument, or writing and programming. Naturally, we do not want to lose focus on these activities when we start them, so worrying will feel less tempting. If we are in a situation where this is not possible, the least we can do is give ourselves a mental task—like reciting a paragraph of our favorite book or doing times tables.

These techniques will only work once we have shut down our urge to worry. We can work, exercise, or do mental math as much as we want, but the only way they will truly engage us is if we do not feel the need to worry anymore.

Not checking in sounds simple enough, but if we have been doing it for a long time, it can be difficult to realize we even are. Luckily, just like panic signals to us that we are worrying, there is one symptom that signals to us that we are checking in: time passes more slowly when we check in, like looking at the clock over and over again during class.

If we feel like time is inching by, it is a sign we are checking in with ourselves too often and should pay special attention to the return step.

In short, after we have answered the suggestive thought, we should focus on step 3: **R**eturn our attention to what we are doing.

MBCT Method: Remind

Once our focus is back on the present, anxious symptoms will begin to fall away on their own. However, even when they are almost gone, our emotional brain will continue to make smaller and less impactful suggestive thoughts about them. When we do not respond to these thoughts, we can feel stuck inside our head, as I have often heard it described.

This brings us to our final step: *remind* ourselves why we do not need to worry. This final step is our way to answer small thoughts without having to repeat the first three steps.

When I say remind, I mean to repeat a short form of our response that immediately shuts down smaller thoughts and lets us get back to what we are doing—something as simple as *Okay, whatever* or *Fine, I don't care*. Once we have reminded ourselves, we return to what is in front of us.

That is the final step of the MBCT process: **R**emind ourselves of our response.

In summary, whenever we hear a suggestive thought coming, we remember the four Rs: **r**ecognize it, **r**espond to it, **r**eturn our focus to what is in front of us, and when smaller thoughts pop up, **r**emind ourselves of our answer. This is a very general guideline for how to apply MBCT, so play around with it to find what works best.

Applied MBCT: Physical Symptoms

I would like to discuss some of the most common anxious symptoms and explain why they happen. This way, whether they arise in social situations or business meetings, during a haircut or an interview, we will be able to answer any suggestive thoughts about them. I also give a few example responses to give you ideas for your own.

Adrenaline Rushes, Trembling, and Twitching

If you have ever had a panic attack, you know exactly what an adrenaline rush feels like. This is the cold flush we get throughout our body, like pins and needles. Usually, adrenaline rushes are followed by trembling and jitters as our body tries to put all of that adrenaline to use.

While adrenaline rushes are the most intense symptom, they are also the easiest to respond to. This is because an adrenaline rush cannot be caused by anything other than our amygdala and will never lead to anything worse; our body can create as much adrenaline as it wants, and we will always be able to dispense of it just fine.[36] When we do not worry about this, it goes away on its own.

As adrenaline starts coursing through our veins and our emotional brain thinks, *Oh no, is this a sign of something horrible?*, we can confidently answer, *No, it'll be fine*, every single time. The shaking, trembling, and twitching are our body's natural way of dispensing its extra adrenaline, so rather than worrying about them, we should welcome them as a sign that our adrenaline levels are going down. Note, these twitches can last for an hour after the adrenaline rush that caused them, so let your body shake it and work on something else.

Shortness of Breath

Shortness of breath is one of the most common symptoms of high adrenaline. When we are short of breath, we sometimes go into manual breathing mode—we worry that, if we do not think, *Breathe in, breathe out,* we will stop breathing. I very distinctly remember sitting on my balcony worrying about this symptom for hours at a time, to the point where I felt like I was drowning out of water. It is a horrible feeling.

Luckily, much like adrenaline rushes, the answer to this suggestive thought is also easy. The part of the brain that controls our breathing, just like the one that makes adrenaline, is out of our control and will keep working without our conscious intervention; no matter how little oxygen we think we are getting, nothing we can do will make our lungs stop breathing.[37] We could try to control this process all day, but even when we stop trying, we continue to breathe normally. In fact, the only way our breathing will return to normal is if we let the brain and lungs do their thing without trying to intervene. This is the benefit of not worrying.

As our breathing returns to normal, we might feel slight tingling or hot flushes. This is a good sign, as it means all of the blood our heart was drawing away from our limbs is getting sent back, meaning we are relaxing out of fight or flight.[38]

If the urge to check on our breath comes back, we can remind ourselves our body will take care of itself, and no amount of checking in will change that. So let yourself feel as out of breath as your body wants for now, then get back to what you were doing.

Case Study: Shortness of Breath and Public Speaking

Worrying about public speaking and the anxious symptoms that come during it are something everyone experiences, but if we have been excessively worrying for many years, our adrenaline levels will be far higher than others'.

One person I spoke to said whenever he was about to present at work, his chest would get tight and he would start to sweat. His emotional brain would ask, *What happens if I screw up because I can't catch my breath?* He started imagining what would happen, causing the symptoms to get even stronger, so when he started talking, it was always between thoughts of *Breathe in, breathe out.*

When we reviewed his history with these symptoms, he saw the way out. As the adrenaline began to flow and his chest felt tight, he recognized the suggestive thought *What if I can't breathe and I have to get rushed to the hospital?* He then responded to them with *Whatever, my coworkers are nice and they will forgive me.* He returned his focus to speaking, and as those suggestive thoughts popped back up, he answered with *Whatever* so he did not panic.

After a few speeches, he found he could answer any thoughts that came, enabling him to focus on his speech the whole way through. Weeks later, he no longer got short of breath at all but knew that, even if he did, he would not worry.

Irregular Heartbeat, High Heart Rate, and Tight Chest

Heart and chest symptoms are where people start to have difficulty—cardiovascular disease is so common in the US these days[39] that having a heart attack is always in the back of our mind. So when our heartbeat becomes irregular and our chest tightens, when our heart rate skyrockets and our heart feels like it is skipping a beat, many of us call an ambulance.

Before we get into how to answer thoughts about this symptom, it is important to clear up a few misconceptions. First, no amount of adrenaline will ever cause heart attack or stroke. This is because the mechanisms behind heart attack and stroke are completely unrelated to worrying and anxious symptoms; they happen when our arteries become blocked by deposits, a process that has everything to do with our diet and nothing to do with our brain.[40] Second, the irregular heartbeats we have are actually harmless. In fact, there is plenty of research that shows completely healthy people experience them, and they have no long-term effect on our health.[41] The technical term for these heartbeats is ectopic beats—not a missed heartbeat as some people believe but an extra one between our normal rhythm. This is our heart's way of making use of all the extra blood it is receiving. Ectopic beats feel like our system is getting a jolt or like a heart hiccup. Lastly, the chest tightness we experience is an effect of adrenaline getting sent to the chest muscles, causing them to flex. This may cause our breathing to become more labored, but it will not cause us to stop breathing.

As we feel our chest tighten, our heart rate increase, and the ectopic beats come, it is important to remind ourselves they are okay and even a welcome presence. The more our body does this, the more adrenaline we are letting out of our system. So when suggestive thoughts arise, we can respond to them and let our body do what it was built to do.

Case Study: Anxious Symptoms at the Gym

One reason people often worry about going to the gym is that there is a lot of overlap between anxious symptoms and physical symptoms of exercise—rapid heartbeat, short breath, sweating, and dizziness just to name a few.

The MBCT response for these situations will be simple, even easier than applying it in other situations: experiencing these symptoms is not a cost at the gym, it is a benefit. The more quickly our heart beats and the faster our breath gets, the better our workout will be. In fact, some exercise methods use heart rate to measure how productive our workout is.[42]

One woman I spoke to initially avoided exercising for this reason. The moment her heart rate increased, she began worrying it was a sign she would have a panic attack and cut her workout short. But as she applied the MBCT method, she grew to like these experiences. She saw the gym as a place to wring out all the adrenaline from her system, which paradoxically caused her body to produce less of it.

Another reason we worry at the gym is we believe people will judge us for the way we are exercising. This thought will not directly lead us to panic, but the symptoms it produces might.

Because the logic behind this worry is not directly related to anxious symptoms, it is best to piece it apart more slowly with CBT, which I cover in the next chapter.

Muscle Tightness and the Throat

During an adrenaline rush, blood gets sent to every muscle in our body more quickly, causing some unexpected areas to tighten. Most often, we recognize this happening in the legs and arms, but the stomach (discussed next) and the throat get tight too. Throat tightness can feel like a physical lump, numbness or itchiness, or difficulty swallowing.

When this symptom happens alongside other anxious symptoms, it is harmless. Many of us worry we will not be able to eat or that we might choke. But as you may have guessed from all of your experiences, throat tightness cannot cause either; high adrenaline can make swallowing difficult, but there is no amount that can make it impossible.[43] If our emotional brain makes thoughts about choking or not finishing our meal, we respond with a *whatever* attitude and focus on something else. Though it will take effort, you will find yourself able to swallow small bits of food, which should encourage you to take bigger and bigger bites.

Throat tightness can, in some rare cases, be tied to other illnesses, but these other illnesses will always come with symptoms unrelated to adrenaline, like a rash or a sore throat. The biggest causes for these are a cold or a mild infection, problems easily addressed by a doctor's appointment. About more serious throat problems we can encounter, like cancer, Barry McDonagh[44] notes even those with throat cancer do not physically feel lumps, and their cancer diagnosis came from other symptoms.

If all of these have been ruled out, the culprit is adrenaline—uncomfortable but harmless.

Tingling Sensation

One function of fight or flight we have not discussed yet is related to blood flow. Specifically, adrenaline causes our body to draw blood away from our extremities and toward our heart and lungs.[45] This is because more blood in our cardiovascular system means more efficient breathing, which leads to better running. One side effect of this is that, as blood is drawn away from our fingers and toes, it results in tingling or numbness. As with all other anxious symptoms, this has no negative effect on our health, so when our emotional brain suggests thoughts about it, we can respond dismissively.

Tingling and numbness occasionally appear in other conditions like diabetes,[46] and while we should definitely check with our doctor if we are concerned, it is not an emergency; if we suspect we might have one of these illnesses, we should schedule an appointment to go through the necessary checkups, but after we make that phone call, we have no need to worry.

There are a few conditions that *do* require immediate action, such as stroke, but in those cases, there is always another accompanying symptom unaffected by adrenaline. For example, the biggest sign of a stroke is muscle paralysis on one half of the body, so people who are having a stroke cannot lift both arms or smile with both sides of their mouth.

Checking for those signs the first time you experience numbness is okay, but if you have experienced it several times before, there is no need to keep checking. And as with all the other symptoms, it will slowly pass when you choose not to worry about it.

Nausea, Vomiting, and Other Stomach Issues

Nausea is one of the more uncomfortable anxious symptoms and is usually the last physical symptom to lighten up during recovery. On the low end, this nausea can cause loss of appetite, but on the high end, it can cause us to dry heave. When most of us already worry about throwing up or not getting a good meal, it should be no wonder nausea is so common.

As unpleasant as it is to be nauseated, our body is fully capable of handling it without our conscious intervention; most waves of nausea come, last for an hour, and go away without any consequences, and throwing up involuntarily is exceedingly rare. However, many of us rush to the restroom and try to throw up when we start to feel nauseated. Doing this is problematic because it robs us of the chance to let our body take care of itself and leads us to throw up even when we do not need to.

Sometimes, we worry about throwing up in public because we think it will be embarrassing. However, I know very few people who have not had to step out in the middle of a meeting or presentation due to illness at least once in their lives, and their coworkers never judged them for it. If we start to actually vomit, we can excuse ourselves to the restroom. However, we must make sure not to do so unless we are actually throwing up.

If this nausea has been present for a few days and we are finding it hard to eat or drink, we should at least try to take small bites and sips throughout the day or drink protein shakes. Forcing down food may feel uncomfortable, but the extra energy will make practicing MBCT (and bringing the nausea to an end) a lot easier.

Adrenaline in the stomach can cause other symptoms, like cramps and irregular bowel movements. While these will also go away as you continue treatment, your doctor is the best one to advise you in the interim.

Insomnia and Anxious Symptoms before Sleep

Another common symptom is difficulty sleeping. This usually stems from one of two causes: worrying in bed and anxious symptoms at night.

As for the first one, I have met so many people who take hours to get to sleep because they feel they cannot turn their brain off. Many of them do not have trouble with anxious symptoms, but they keep themselves up worrying about what happened that day or about uncomfortable memories.

Typically, this kind of nonpanic worrying is best addressed through CBT, but sleeping is a special case. When we are home in bed, the answer to *Should I worry about this right now?* is always no; none of the worrying we do in bed ever leads us to take action, so it is nothing more than a waste of time and energy.

If we have a particular problem on our mind, we can write it down and tackle it after we wake up. But no matter how badly we feel like we need to worry, we will always do it better after a full night's sleep.

As suggestive thoughts arise, we can use the four Rs. In the response step, we can give all of these thoughts the same answer: *I will take care of it tomorrow.*

Here, there is some nuance to the return step as well: if we are trying to go to sleep, the last thing we want to do is get out of bed and start doing something productive. Instead, we can meditate. When done properly, meditation gives us something to return to without needing to move around and can be done lying down with our eyes closed. If you would like to know more about meditation, check the lifestyle changes section.

Poor sleep can also be caused by anxious symptoms at night—we worry about what will happen if we do not sleep, causing the symptoms we experience to become stronger and keep us up for longer. Here, it helps to know that, while sleep is important for our *overall* health, a single or even multiple nights of poor sleep are not enough to cause significant lasting damage.[47] The following day may be uncomfortable, but there is no reason to worry about it. If our concern is with social situations, remember that everyone knows what it is like to sleep poorly, and no one will judge you for it.

For these reasons, Barry McDonagh[48] recommends really being at peace with the idea of not sleeping at all. Like giving up a tug of war with yourself. Counterintuitively, this gives your body the chance to finally relax and actually get to sleep.

On a final note, I have some tips for maintaining sleep hygiene in the lifestyle changes section.

Hypnic Jerks

If we are going through a long period of high adrenaline, we may experience hypnic jerks[49]—a falling feeling, full-body spasm, ectopic beat, or a punch to the gut right as we go to sleep.

The medical community is not sure why this happens, but one of the more common theories is that it is our brain's way of getting ready to shut down; before we go unconscious, our body needs to make sure we will not move around during sleep, and so it slowly relaxes its muscles into a state of paralysis. After a little while, our brain sends a test signal to check whether our muscles are fully paralyzed—a pulse to make our muscles shake to test whether they still can. If this signal reaches the muscles and they are shut off, nothing happens and we go to sleep. But if they are still on, it results in a single, full-body twitch, which causes us to wake up. This happens to everyone occasionally but more frequently to those of us in a period of high adrenaline.[50]

As with all the other symptoms, hypnic jerks are harmless; they only happen as a result of high adrenaline levels or by random chance, not any other health condition. We can answer any suggestive thoughts that arise about these hypnic jerks using the four Rs, with special attention to the previous section about sleep.

When my adrenaline first peaked, I had to endure some of the worst sleep I have ever gotten. Every time I fell asleep, my body would jerk me awake after twenty minutes, but the worrying I did after caused me to get less than an hour of sleep total. Once I began to respond to my suggestive thoughts, the hypnic jerks stopped escalating into panic, and no matter how often I woke up, I was able to get right back to sleep. Twenty-minute bursts of sleep very quickly turned into one- and two-hour-long ones, and after a week and a half, I was only waking up once if at all.

Dizziness and Fainting Feeling

When our adrenaline levels are high, we can experience dizziness that is difficult to explain. When ear, nose, and throat doctors check us for signs of vertigo, another kind of dizziness, they often ask whether it feels like the world is spinning around us, or if it feels like we are spinning.[51] When this dizziness is caused by adrenaline, it does not feel like either. If our adrenaline levels are especially high, it can cause small bursts so intense that we feel like we could faint. This can be scary, especially when we are in social situations. But as you may have gathered, adrenaline cannot actually cause us to faint.

One reason for fainting is our blood vessels expanding rapidly, like when we stand up too quickly. When this happens, the brain does not receive enough blood, so we lose consciousness.[52] However, adrenaline causes our blood vessels to *contract*, not expand, meaning rather than make us faint, adrenaline actually *prevents* it.

Another common reason why people faint is dehydration or lack of electrolytes. Our body has a broad range of how much water and salt it needs—salts carry charge throughout our body, and this can only happen when they are suspended in enough water. When we have too little of either, our heart and brain become unable to send and receive signals, also resulting in loss of consciousness.[53] However, this is rare. If we are drinking water whenever we feel thirsty, are occasionally snacking on something salty, and are not in the middle of the desert, we are not going to faint.

The reason why adrenaline causes dizziness is not fully understood, but there are two major theories. The first is that dizziness is a side effect of tense neck muscles—these muscles are involved in balance, and when adrenaline tightens them, we feel off-balance.[54] The second is that adrenaline can affect the nerves in our vestibular system, the part of the brain in charge of balance.[55] In both cases, adrenaline can cause discomfort but not fainting. So the best thing we can do is let it be there without worrying about it, and it will go away on its own time.

Case Study: Fainting Feeling and Performances

Everyone has had to deal with anxious symptoms before a performance. Most often, these symptoms come because we worry about performing well, which causes our cortex to activate our amygdala.

This can happen before onstage performances, but it can happen offstage as well. One woman I worked with experienced anxious symptoms whenever she sat down to take a test. Her heart raced, she got dizzy, and her emotional brain produced thoughts about fainting. She worried about this, causing her symptoms to get worse, until after a minute, she hit full-blown panic in the middle of her test.

Her answer came when she recognized she had not fainted or even failed a test even once, despite how uncomfortable she felt. She was always able to work through dizziness and perform well despite it. This formed the basis for the response and reminder she used: *I know it'll be fine. It always has been.*

As she got better at answering suggestive thoughts about fainting, she began to like these adrenaline rushes; she told herself, *This is just extra energy I can channel into taking my test.* After a few tests, she no longer experienced panic, and a few weeks later, the symptoms stopped coming entirely.

Headaches

One anxious symptom few people are aware of is headaches. Headaches have several causes, but one of the most common ones is tension in the back of the neck.[57] Our neck muscles connect to muscles in our face, so when our neck gets strained, the pain can pop up behind our eyes. There are many reasons why our neck muscles can get tense, but as you read earlier, one of these reasons is adrenaline. This means that those of us in a period of high adrenaline will experience more frequent, more intense, and longer headaches.

While the tension in our muscles will go down as we recover, there are a few other ways we can make our neck more resilient. The first is by stretching it out a few times a day. This helps our muscles become more elastic and prevents damage.[57] The second is by keeping our muscles in a position that will not strain them. In other words, by maintaining proper posture. This means keeping our neck in a straight line with our back, perpendicular to the ground, with our chin parallel.[58]

Much like any other change, choosing to stretch and fix our posture will be uncomfortable at first, but we get used to it within a few weeks.

As a side note, headaches can also happen when we are dehydrated,[59] so we should make sure we are drinking enough water. If we have worked on our posture and muscle strength for a few weeks without any improvement in our headaches, or we experience visual symptoms like in migraines, it never hurts to consult a doctor. Headaches can come from other sources, though these are also highly treatable.[60]

Vision and Hearing

Vision and hearing issues can also arise during a period of high adrenaline, though they are not often discussed. During fight or flight, our brain needs to be able to take in as much information as possible, so it enters a state of hyper-awareness; adrenaline causes our pupils to dilate and become more sensitive to movement, leading small things moving out of the corner of our eyes (or even not moving at all) to catch our attention more often.[61]

In addition, it causes us to see eye floaters—loose fibers that have broken up within our eye—more frequently. Floaters are normally invisible, but when our pupils dilate, they are exposed to more light, causing the floaters' shadows to become visible.[62] This happens to everyone occasionally, but if our pupils dilate more often, as they do in a period of high adrenaline, we will see them more frequently.

Adrenaline also causes the ears to become more sensitive, helping them pick up more noise. This can cause everyday noises to feel painfully loud, especially when the rest of our surroundings are quiet, and can make us overly jumpy.[62]

People sometimes misinterpret these symptoms as a sign of another mental health condition, but this is not the case. They are a normal effect of adrenaline and will lighten up throughout our recovery.

Sexual Dysfunction

The last physical symptom I would like to discuss is decreased sexual function.

The reason adrenaline decreases sexual function was touched upon earlier: during fight or flight, blood is drawn toward our heart and away from extremities, including the sex organs. This makes it more difficult to become physically aroused, especially for men.[63] In addition, worrying about anxious symptoms can make it difficult to concentrate on sex.

When we understand where this symptom comes from, it becomes easier to let it be present for a few minutes and then slowly pass. However, if we keep asking ourselves whether we are able to perform, eventually this worrying will be enough to make the answer no. This is why the return step is especially important.

There are other factors that can contribute to sexual dysfunction, like age or other preexisting conditions.[64] If you have been practicing MBCT for a month without seeing progress, you can always ask your doctor.

Applied MBCT: Mental Symptoms

Mental symptoms are milder than physical ones, but they also tend to give people more trouble because they are much harder to rationalize—when we have the jitters or nausea, we can easily point the finger at adrenaline. But when we suddenly feel disconnected from our surroundings, and thoughts of going crazy pop into our head, it is much harder to make sense of what is going on. In the following chapter, I will review the most common mental symptoms of high adrenaline to help you respond to them.

Depersonalization

Of all the anxious symptoms I have experienced, depersonalization (DP) was the hardest to explain. Each person experiences it a little differently, but is often described as feeling like you are a passenger in your own body, seeing your arms from the third person, being mentally and emotionally detached from your surroundings, or having a delay between what you see and your thoughts about it. Trying to explain this to someone who has never experienced it can feel impossible, and when no one seems to have an answer, we can mistakenly believe we are going crazy (which I discuss next).

The exact mechanism behind DP is not yet known, but the most prominent theory states that having an abundance of adrenaline (leading to an abundance of anxious symptoms) dulls our ability to process each individual one[65]—when our emotional brain is trying to bring too many sights, sounds, smells, and tastes to our attention at once, our conscious brain compensates by shutting certain ones out, leading to a feeling of detachment.

As frightening as depersonalization may seem at first, it can only come as a result of adrenaline overload and not from any other condition. And as you have noticed, it does not lead to any other mental conditions, nor even affect our behavior, so we have no reason to worry about it.

Though it may be difficult to imagine, many people come to enjoy depersonalization when they stop worrying about it as there is nothing inherently bad about feeling disconnected. In fact, experienced during a drug trip, many find this sensation relaxing.

Adopting this same positive attitude will prevent DP from sticking around and eventually get it to go away.

Thoughts and Feelings of Going Crazy

While DP might be the strangest symptom, the feeling of going crazy is the one that gives people the most trouble. Even in the middle of crippling nausea, vomiting, or insomnia, many of us still find the thought of losing our mind to be the most important. In my first weeks of treatment, I spent hours each day researching the symptoms of bipolar disorder and schizophrenia to check if I was having a mental break.

To make matters worse, there is such a stigma around psychotic illnesses that it makes the topic unapproachable to most people. Empathizing with physical symptoms like nausea and insomnia is easy because all of us have felt them at some point in our lives. But thoughts of going crazy only become noticeable to people with high adrenaline levels. For this reason, so many of us feel like we have to keep these thoughts secret—to suffer in silence—which makes our experience with them so much worse. If you are going through the same thing right now, I feel for you.

As difficult as it might be to imagine, the key to getting rid of this symptom is in our hands, just like all of the others—understanding why it happens and how to stop worrying about it.

Thoughts of going crazy originate from the part of our brain that creates all of our suggestive thoughts: the emotional brain, which produces thousands of suggestive thoughts and emotions each day about a range of topics.[66] As mentioned earlier, the emotional brain can be energized by adrenaline, which causes it to produce thoughts more quickly, especially ones that come with a sense of urgency.

One such thought that everyone's emotional brain has occasionally (even those who are not going through a period of high adrenaline) is *What if I'm going crazy?* Those who do not regularly worry about this topic will usually ignore it because they do not value worrying about it. But if we do, our worrying creates more adrenaline, causing that thought to come even harder. In addition, our emotional brain takes this to mean the thought was helpful, and so it starts to create the thought more often, even when we wish it would not.

In this situation, the emotional brain is not the issue—the suggestive thoughts it creates only pop up for a split second and go away when we choose not to worry about them. The real issue is the worrying we do afterward, signaling to the brain to keep making these thoughts and supplying it with more adrenaline.

This brings up an important point. The feeling of going crazy can actually be broken up into two things: the thoughts our brain produces and our worrying about them. As with all other anxious symptoms, when we stop worrying, this symptom fades away on its own.

So how do we respond to such a frightening thought? The answer lies in knowing more about psychotic illnesses.

As difficult as it may be to believe, the *thoughts* of going crazy and *actually* having a psychotic episode are not only two totally different symptoms but many psychiatrists believe we cannot experience both at the same time.[67]

One of the theories of schizophrenia, the most common psychotic disorder, is that it happens because a part of the prefrontal cortex (the conscious cortex) does not develop correctly—a problem that starts in young adulthood and *very slowly* gets worse. Eventually, this makes them unable to consider new information deeply.[68]

Practically, this means that when asked questions like *Am I going crazy?* or *What if I embarrass myself?* or *Am I acting out right now?*, people with aggressive schizophrenia are not capable of weighing the information well enough to answer yes or no. In fact, when they experience a psychotic episode, they hardly realize they are acting out at all.[69] This is what has led to the old adage within the psychological community: "If you feel like you are going crazy, you probably aren't."[67]

For this reason, when professionals diagnose a psychotic illness, they do not look at symptoms their patient is experiencing when they get to the hospital. Instead, they look at their patient's behavior—their ability to answer simple questions and their awareness of their surroundings—as well as their history with psychotic episodes.[70] For them, the difference between anxious symptoms and a psychotic illness is night and day. This is why we can *only* be diagnosed by a psychologist or psychiatrist, and if they say it is just anxious symptoms, we must trust their word, even over our own emotional brain's suggestions.

If we are still feeling unsure, and the idea of having such a mental disorder scares us, we can remember that many people experience occasional psychotic symptoms like brief hallucinations or mood swings, but they come infrequently. As a result, these symptoms do not intrude on their lives, and they do not ever need to get formally diagnosed and treated.

Of those who do experience strong symptoms, many are able to treat them with medication and go on to lead comfortable and happy lives.

Studies are even beginning to show that some people can eventually taper off the medication without having another psychotic episode.[71]

With all of this information in mind, we really have no reason to worry. If we have not been diagnosed with a psychotic illness, we do not have one, and even if we do, the odds are overwhelmingly positive that it will not majorly affect us.

Our response to these thoughts will be highly personal, but I found two specific responses helpful for this. The first was that I had experienced these same thoughts for months and had not yet gone crazy. If it did not happen yesterday, last week, last month, or last year, it would not happen today. The second was that, no matter what I felt, I could not diagnose myself because psychotic illnesses cannot be self-diagnosed. And as I had seen hundreds of times, my diagnoses always ended up wrong anyway.

With thoughts of going crazy, the return step is especially important. If we respond to a suggestive thought, only to ask ourselves *Am I going crazy?* the next second, we will go back to looking for symptoms. The only way to win the game of *Am I going crazy?* is not to play at all—to respond so dismissively that we do not even need an answer.

Case Study: Thoughts of Going Crazy and Public Speaking

Like many people I worked with, one man who contacted me responded well to physical symptoms but had trouble with thoughts of going crazy. He was okay dismissing the thoughts when he was by himself, but the minutes before he left the house for work, he began to worry about them. This caused them to stick around throughout the day until he got home and unwound.

The breakthrough point for him came when he realized he had never actually gone crazy, despite thinking about it for several hundred hours. Not only that, he realized that if he ever did go through a moment of "craziness," he could always just catch himself, apologize, and move on. When he learned about how psychotic illnesses work, he began to feel he had nothing to be afraid of.

Thus, when thoughts of going crazy came up, he responded by telling himself, *If I go crazy, so be it. I know it'll be no problem.* When the thoughts popped up again, he responded with, *Not happening,* and got back to business. After a few weeks of this response, he no longer worried about them anymore. In the month after, they went away almost entirely.

I personally spent months figuring out how to respond to these thoughts. If you are in the same boat, remember that, as long as you keep looking for an answer, it is just a matter of time before you find it.

Racing, Intrusive Thoughts

Thoughts of going crazy are some of the most common uncomfortable thoughts our emotional brain can make, but they are not the only ones. It can make thoughts that are violent—about driving our car off the road, stabbing our partner, screaming out in class, our family dying in an accident, or of committing suicide in a moment of psychosis. These thoughts can also be nonsensical, indescribable, or unreal—a brief flash of an image so bizarre and unrelated to what we are doing, we cannot explain it in words. These thoughts pop up all the time, but the only ones that we notice are those that resonate with us—thoughts about our friends and family, our religion, our sexuality, and our personal health, to name a few. For the longest time, I was afraid to discuss these thoughts with anyone, even my therapist, in case I really was crazy.

As explained above, intrusive thoughts happen as a result of our emotional brain receiving adrenaline. When it does, it not only produces thoughts that are more intense, but also ones that are less appropriate to our situation. This is why they are called intrusive thoughts—they are unhelpful and unwelcome.

However, as you now know, the part of the brain that *creates* thoughts and the one that *decides what to do with them* are separate. An unhealthy brain is one that is not capable of reacting to them at all. If we recognize these thoughts and can make a choice to either ignore them or think further, it means our brain is healthy.

In truth, everyone has bizzare and nonsensical thoughts from time to time. We do not often talk about it, but the sudden urge to scream out in a meeting or randomly drive off the freeway is totally normal, as weird as it may seem. In fact, the French have a phrase for it: l'appel du vide—the call of the void—the urge to do something violent or depraved, but with the choice to never act on it. If just having these thoughts meant we would act on them, our business meetings and freeways would look much different.

Those who do not worry about their health choose to ignore intrusive thoughts when they come up, so they slip by without a problem. When we do worry, however, it leads our body to make adrenaline, causing these thoughts to come up more often and more intensely. The way we fix this is by doing what the others do: let them come and go without checking for their presence, using the four Rs as our method.

If we have gotten to the point where we can handle all other physical and mental symptoms besides intrusive thoughts, it is a sign we are getting close to full recovery. Thoughts take much less adrenaline to produce than symptoms like nausea and jitters, so if they are our only problem, it means our adrenaline levels are almost back to normal.

Case Study: Intrusive Thoughts and Worrying about Flying

Worrying about flying is quite common and with good reason—airplanes are loud and uncomfortable, and when news of a crash comes out every few years, we can easily get fooled into thinking they are unsafe.

One woman who approached me experienced severe anxious symptoms when flying. She said that, in the hours before she boarded a plane, she would get hit with thoughts about having a panic attack in the air. Then, during takeoff and landing, thoughts of a plane crash came up, and her worrying about them caused waves of nausea and vomiting that would leave her uncomfortable for the rest of the week.

Her recovery began with a look at her past experience with flying, as well as some statistics. She found that, as much as she worried about her plane crashing, she had never even experienced an emergency landing. As she learned, flying is actually safer than most other things we do every day, like driving a car, working in an office, or going shopping. Even though the anxious symptoms that arose during flying made her uncomfortable, they did not have actual consequences.

Armed with that knowledge, we made a plan of action. When she reached the airport, she knew her adrenaline would start pumping, so she committed to answering the thoughts that came up with *So be it, I guess I'll just be uncomfortable for now*. She then shifted her focus to her laptop or games console as her return step.

As she entered the plane and prepared for takeoff (and landing later on), the thoughts of crashing came, so she answered them with *Whatever, I know it's not going to happen* and shifted her attention to a podcast.

By following this plan, she found that, on her very next plane ride, her anxious symptoms peaked at a much lower level and remained for much less time. Within a few plane rides, she found she was so comfortable with the thoughts and symptoms that came up that she could look out the window without worrying.

While it would be ideal if we could always confront scary situations directly, some of us would rather do so more gradually. If this resonates with you, check out the ERP chapter.

Compulsion and Avoidance Urges

This brings us to the last danger-focused thought the emotional brain makes: urges to behave unhealthily. The urge can be about compulsions or avoidance—to keep washing our hands until it hurts or to stay away from certain situations. But it can also be much simpler—the urge to check in with ourselves or to worry.

While these might not feel normal, they are the way our brain is supposed to react—our emotional brain senses us acting in a way we are not used to, and not knowing any better, it suggests we should stop.

To find the most meaningful response, we can look at our valuations. Most often, we act on urges because we do not want to experience the discomfort of stopping. But when we remind ourselves that this discomfort is temporary, productive, and to be expected, it becomes much easier to answer them with a so-be-it attitude.

One idea I find helpful is looking at it like exercise. When we first start applying MBCT, even a little response will feel uncomfortable, but the more we do it, the more we will be able to handle. In time, this practice will make those urges quieter and quieter until they reach total silence.

If we have been worrying for a long time, this silence may feel strange—as if there is something we should be thinking about but are not. New thoughts will pop up tempting us to worry again, like *What if I don't check my body and that symptom comes back?* or *What if I stop thinking about everything I say and I embarrass myself?* Such thoughts are trickier so it will take some experimentation to understand how to answer them convincingly. But like other intrusive thoughts, they will get weaker the less time we spend worrying about them.

Brain Fog and Difficulty Concentrating

This concludes the most serious mental symptoms. If we are capable of experiencing DP and intrusive suggestive thoughts without worrying, it means we are in the final stage of recovery: mild mental symptoms. The most common of these is brain fog—the feeling of not being able to think clearly, of having problems with short-term memory, and of not being able to focus. For me, brain fog felt like a brick wall in front of my thoughts, preventing me from thinking about them for too long.

Brain fog, like many other symptoms, happens when our emotional brain is energized.[72] When this happens, it creates thoughts more quickly and brings them to our attention more often, making it difficult to focus on anything else.

This is one symptom everyone can be sympathetic toward; poor sleep or diet, uncomfortable temperatures, a night of drinking, and a whole host of other factors have caused everyone to feel hazy at least once in their lives. Right now, adrenaline is causing this feeling frequently, but even once you fully recover, it is okay for you to feel unfocused. This can form the core of your response.

Emotions

Another symptom that we can experience toward the end of our recovery has to do with our emotions. When we have high adrenaline, anxious symptoms become so strong that our emotions feel muted.[73] In situations where other people might feel happy, we find it hard to feel anything. For some, this feels like sadness, but for others it feels like depressive symptoms—emptiness or listlessness. Usually, this feeling clears up as we progress through treatment.

Depressive symptoms can also arise for another reason, one that is similar to worrying and anxious symptoms: when we respond to suggestive thoughts by ruminating (spending excessive amounts of time thinking about negative events in the future), it dials down the production of certain hormones, leading to a feeling of emptiness. Like worrying, ruminating is unproductive and is indicative of unbalanced valuations.

Many of us not only worry about our anxious symptoms, we ruminate on them, causing depressive symptoms. The good news is that, in all of these situations, the treatment is the same: CBT (discussed in the next section). When we understand the damage of rumination, we can stop engaging in it (as we do with worrying), leading symptoms to eventually go away. Since you will practice CBT in the next section, you will have a chance to tackle both problems at the same time.

There is another caveat to emotions during recovery. Once our adrenaline levels are low enough, our emotions start to come back. At first, this may feel overwhelming—when we are not used to feeling happy, sad, or angry, it may feel like we are *overly* emotional. Though most people do not worry about this, those of us who do can respond like we do to anxious symptoms: we know emotions are not a bad thing, so we do not need to worry about them. In time, they level out and we come to enjoy them.

Fatigue

The very final symptom we will discuss in this book is fatigue—sluggishness or drowsiness. Even when we no longer have any other physical or mental symptoms and our emotions have all returned, we can feel tired.

The full mechanism behind this has not been uncovered yet, but I believe it has to do with how much energy our body uses during a period of high adrenaline. When our body has to maintain a high heart rate, rapid breathing, and fast digestion for an extended period of time, we will have much less energy left over for anything else. Coupled with the negative effect of high adrenaline on sleep quality, it only makes sense that we will feel fatigued.

Luckily, when we stop worrying, we stop fueling these symptoms, leaving more energy available for us to use. Fatigue will gradually fade away as we worry less and less, though it may take a little longer to dissipate than other symptoms.

Applied MBCT: General Advice

Now, that we understand the theory behind MBCT, we can put it into action. One thing to keep in mind is that we will not start out being able to apply it perfectly; there will be times when we recognize we are falling into the spiral but cannot find a good response. This is to be expected, especially in the beginning. Building new synaptic pathways is like building muscles, and even the biggest and strongest weightlifters in the world did not start out lifting Atlas stones. The key, like with exercise, is to keep at it and focus on gradual improvement. If you are looking for a recovery roadmap, check out the later sections.

One concern I hear often is about what we should do if we suspect a symptom is caused by something other than adrenaline. For the vast majority of health issues, it is recommended we visit the doctor after only a week of experiencing a new symptom. If an issue has not gotten any better and over-the-counter medication is not helping, we can schedule an appointment to get all the necessary medical checkups. But take it from me, if all the doctors are saying you are clear, trust them.

In my early 20s, I worried so much about my health that I went to at least ten different *kinds* of doctors: GPs, neurologists, ENTs, cardiologists, radiologists, audiologists, pain specialists, allergists, and eastern medicine practitioners. Unfortunately, since I spent so much time googling my anxious symptoms, I was convinced I had some rare condition like fibromyalgia or vestibular migraines. But after all of the tests came back, I was left with a clean bill of health.

Had I been allowed to follow my intuition on every one of my self-diagnoses, I would currently be going through chemotherapy, recovering from a septoplasty, getting allergy shots, taking tons of prescription medications for neurological disorders, and still worrying just as often and experiencing all of the same symptoms. If this sounds familiar, read on to the CBT section.

Along these same lines, many of us are held back by our desire for the symptoms to go away rather than stick around—we might start therapy with the intention of never experiencing anxious symptoms again. But doing this is like trying to lose weight without the discomfort of dieting; our brain and body will not change unless we apply stress to them by doing things that are uncomfortable.

Lastly, if you have not yet found the answers that work for you and want more ideas of what applied MBCT looks like, I have a few suggestions in the recommended reading section. While they do not explain *why* MBCT works, they explain how to apply it. Now that you have read this book, you will be able to modify those methods to better fit you.

COGNITIVE BEHAVIORAL THERAPY

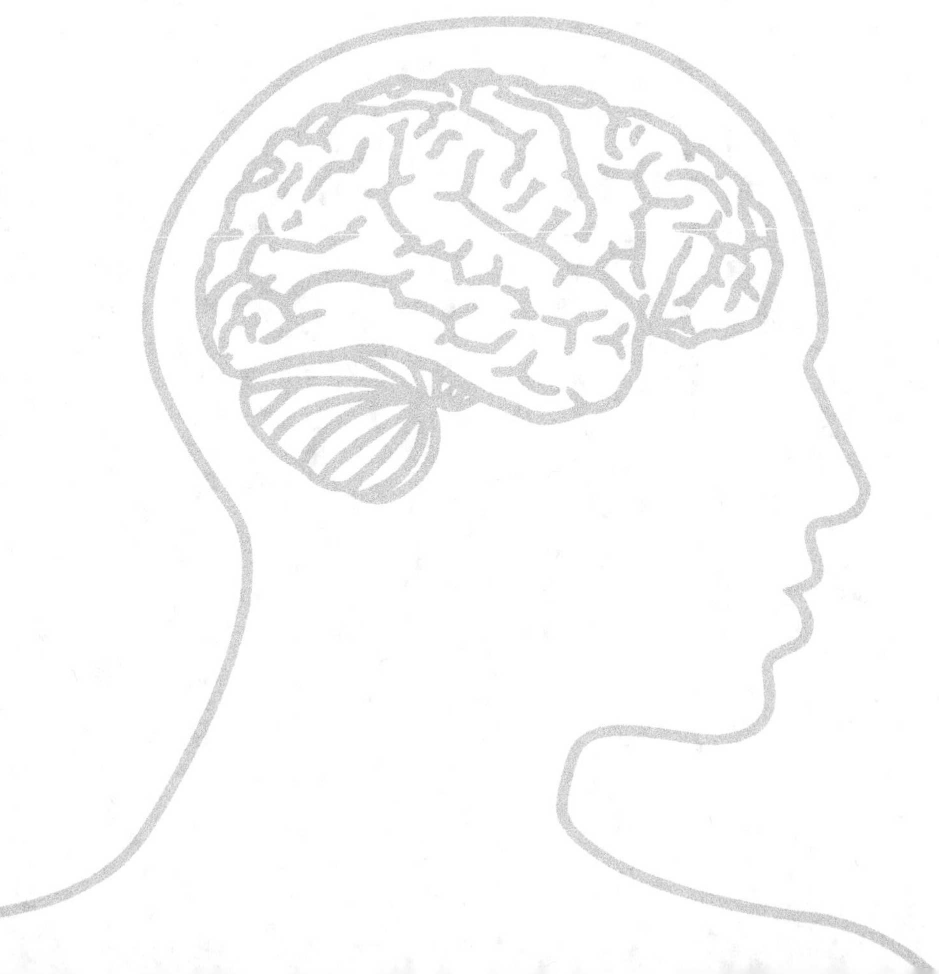

The CBT Method to Curb Conscious Worrying

Now that we understand MBCT, we have all the tools we need to stop worrying about anxious symptoms. We learned that, in almost all cases, worrying about these symptoms is not worth the time and the discomfort it leads to. And in the exceedingly rare case that our symptoms are due to another condition, we learned how to tell the difference so that we can take appropriate action.

However, unlike worrying about anxious symptoms, worrying about other subjects *can* be worth the time and lead us to act productively—situations in which *Whatever, so be it* is not the best approach. This is especially true for relationships, finances, and our career. For this reason, we need a method to identify what worrying is helpful and what is unhelpful. This is the purpose of CBT.

Theory: Helpful, Productive Worrying

To differentiate between healthy and unhealthy worrying, we can use one hard and fast rule: healthy worrying is *efficient* and *actionable*, while unhealthy worrying is *inefficient, inactionable,* or both.

Here, efficient means we spend no more than a few minutes considering a thought. Actionable means this consideration leads us to take meaningful action. Like we touched upon earlier, brief worrying about our finances can lead us to budget for the month. Or brief worrying about our weight can lead us to plan a diet.

This worrying is healthy because it takes little time, and since it helps us solve a problem in a timely manner, it is a one-off activity. Thus, when we notice ourselves doing this kind of worrying, the solution is simple: act on it when we can, and dog-ear—mark it for later on our phone or calendar—when we cannot.

Theory: Unhelpful, Unproductive Worrying

For most of us, this kind of worrying is not the default. Instead, we spend most of our time worrying for hours without any intention of acting—worrying in a way that is *inefficient* and *inactionable*. We may worry for hours about a social event without even getting out of our chair. Or we may worry about our health for months until we finally go to a doctor, and keep worrying even once our test results come back negative.

Because this worrying does not lead us to act in meaningful ways, we can worry about the same thing over and over again—for many months or years—without getting any closer to a solution. If our valuations were realistic, we would stop worrying once we realize it does not benefit us. The fact that we do not tells us one of our valuations is unrealistic.

Theory: Psychological Change

As discussed earlier, the way our valuations get so bent out of shape is because of conditioning. After worrying in an illogical or excessive way a few times, we begin to become more comfortable with it. If we continue, we can become so comfortable that we do not realize how much it is actually hurting us—we become cognitively blind.

To demonstrate, ask yourself these questions. How many times have you worried about something that ended up being a false alarm, only to fall for the same trap the next time? How many flights have you taken where you were convinced your plane was going to crash, only to land safely? How much of your time socializing with others was spent worrying about how to act, only to end without you saying or doing a single embarrassing thing? If you are like me, the answer is "Enough that I would rather not think about it."

CBT was designed to address this—to help us look at our valuations, analyze how realistic they are, and change them so we choose to worry less.

The CBT Response

In the context of this book, I will focus on using CBT to change valuations that cause us to worry. However, we can apply it to any valuations we believe are unrealistic, like those that cause us to ruminate.

The CBT process starts when we find ourselves worrying inefficiently or inactionably. When we become aware we are doing this, we start the first step: **recognize** what we are worrying about. Just like MBCT, we can do this by asking ourselves *What am I worrying about?*, so long as our answer spells it out clearly and specifically.

The second step helps us pinpoint a valuation that is causing us to worry in this way. To do this, we can **answer** the question, *Why am I worrying about this?*

The third step, **assess**, is the defining step of CBT. In this step, we examine the logic in our valuation to see why it is unrealistic. There are hundreds of logical fallacies we can look at to accomplish this, but long-time practitioner of CBT David Burns has identified a core group of fallacies that most of us engage in, which he calls cognitive distortions. If we look at this list, odds are we will find at least one way our valuations are unrealistic. If nothing about our answer sticks out at us, we can return to the previous step and ask *Why am I worrying about this answer?*, then find the distortion in our new answer.

Once we have chosen a distortion, the last step of CBT is to **counter** our old valuation with one that is more logical. This way, it will become easier to use that valuation next time we need to.

In short, the CBT method is *recognize* the thought we are worrying about, *answer* why we are worrying about it, *assess* the strength of our logic, and *counter* it with something more logical.

Much like MBCT, the CBT response can be practiced entirely in our head. However, since it is more complex, some people like to jot down their ideas in a journal or a workbook or have their therapist keep track.

Now that we have reviewed how to apply the CBT method, we can examine the different cognitive distortions.

CBT Methods: Cognitive Distortions and Case Studies

In this chapter, I will explain the most common cognitive distortions. After each explanation, I will give an example of a person who I have worked with on this distortion, as well as the CBT response they used.

Since there are many cognitive distortions to read through, the best way to use this chapter is to choose one or two that resonate with you and read them through. To do this, you can read the topic sentence of each section where I define the distortion.

As a final note, keep in mind that CBT problems have no correct answer. The way in which you analyze the following case studies or the cognitive distortion you assign to them might be different from me or your therapist or David Burns. The goal of CBT is not to apply it perfectly but rather to keep asking ourselves how we can be more realistic.

Black-and-White Thinking and Perfectionism

Black-and-white thinking is usually the first cognitive distortion discussed in CBT because it is the easiest to understand. Thinking in black and white means assuming that all situations have two outcomes: good or bad, positive or negative.

This way of thinking is harmful because our lives are too complex and subjective to be thought of in such simple terms; we cannot say eating food or having a conversation is good, nor that playing games or going to sleep is bad. If we assign these labels to them, we risk giving unnecessary meaning to neutral experiences; when we label a hard workout as bad, it only leads us to avoid it in the future, when hard workouts are really just normal. If we label going and drinking with friends good, when really it is okay sometimes and not okay other times, we will do it even when it hurts us.

To demonstrate what black-and-white valuation looks like, I would like to use myself as an example. My problems with black-and-white valuations started at a young age and were focused on a single topic: my health. I worried almost every day about getting sick.

When I was finally introduced to CBT, I learned to examine why I thought this way, and why it was unrealistic:

1. I recognized my thought by asking *What am I worrying about?* I responded with "I am worrying about feeling sick."

2. I asked myself, *Why am I worrying about being sick?* My response was "I am worrying because being sick feels uncomfortable." I could not find anything wrong with the logic here, so I asked myself, *Why am I worrying about feeling uncomfortable?* My response was "Being uncomfortable is bad."

3. I assessed this valuation by asking, *Is this objectively true? Could this be the black-and-white-thinking fallacy? Is feeling uncomfortable always bad? Can it be "not that bad" or even neutral?*

4. Last, I countered that valuation with one that was more helpful. I said, "Feeling uncomfortable and being sick is not the end of the world. Even people with chronic conditions that make them uncomfortable can find relief through medication and live a happy life."

Within a few weeks of picking apart my thoughts like this, the value I put on avoiding discomfort and being sick began to decrease. As a byproduct, I stopped worrying about my health, googling my symptoms, and spending time asking myself whether I should go to the doctor.

Good and bad are not the only way we can mislabel things. A few other common black-and-white valuations are success and failure, right and wrong, good and evil, winner and loser, smart and stupid, beautiful and ugly, normal and abnormal, and these days especially, *perfect and imperfect.*

Much like other black-and-white fallacies, perfectionism fails us because it is too simple and subjective; what we think is perfect may not seem so to others. Not only that, it sets our expectations so high that meeting them is impossible. This leads us to spend large amounts of time on one project when we could be doing several—a much more efficient and productive use of our time.

For this reason, rather than striving for perfectionism, David Burns recommends trying to be average for a day and seeing where it gets you. That is, rather than striving for perfect work, try just being good enough. If you are interested in a deeper dive into perfectionism, I highly recommend his book *Feeling Good: The New Mood Therapy.*

Unproductive Metrics and Low Self-Esteem

Before we discuss what metrics are productive and unproductive, we have to understand what a metric is. In the hard sciences, metrics are ways in which we objectively measure and compare things: weight, volume, pressure, etc. These metrics are objective because no matter how we measure them, our answer will always be the same.

Our valuations, however, cannot be measured objectively. Instead, we have to choose how we measure them. For example, we can value our hobby based on how much money it makes us, how much fun we have, or how much it influences other people. As you can guess, some of these metrics are healthy and realistic, while others are not and lead us to excessively worry.

An example of this is in one young man who approached me worrying about his self-worth. He had just graduated from college with a degree in business and, after several interviews, had failed to land a high paying job like his friends.

He often worried about what this meant for his value as a person. He would ask himself whether he was worthless for not having a high-paying job, leading him to feel guilty.

Together, we worked to understand why he did so and how to change it:

> **R**: I am worrying that not having a high-paying job makes me worthless.
>
> **A**: The reason is that we need to have money to be worth anything.
>
> **A**: Am I using an unproductive metric in my valuation? Is money really a good way to measure people's worth? Are there people who are worth a lot to me who do not make a lot of money?
>
> **C**: My teachers, counselors, and coaches all made the biggest difference in my life. They were worth the most to me, even though they did not make a lot of money. Maybe I should use a different metric to value myself, like how much of a positive impact I make on others. Or maybe I can choose to value everyone equally. That way, I won't value my salary as much in my decisions.

By changing the metrics he used, this man found himself valuing money less, leading him to spend less time worrying about how much he made and more time thinking about how he could help others. After a short while, he began reaching out to his friends and family more often and making a more positive impact in their lives.

I know self-esteem is something a lot of us struggle with; when we are in a period of high adrenaline, it can be difficult to focus on anything outside of our body, so many of us mistakenly believe this makes us worth less than others. Of course, measuring our self-worth by how much we can overextend ourselves to help others during our recovery is unhealthy, but I know many people who still feel guilty about it.

If you are someone who values helping people and cannot right now, you can boost your self-worth with a pact. You know that extending yourself too much during your recovery will be unhelpful, so when you feel better, you will help others more than you did before. If you want to get a head start, you can do little things, like give money to someone in need, compliment someone, or show support to someone who is struggling. You might be surprised just how impactful small gestures are and how much better you will feel about yourself afterward.

Magnification (Catastrophizing)

Magnification, also known as catastrophizing, means overvaluing the worst-case scenario. For example, if we are about to have surgery, magnifying would mean worrying about what happens if it goes catastrophically wrong. Or if we are about to take a test, it would mean worrying about what would happen if we fail.

Magnifying is problematic because these worst-case scenarios almost never happen; usually, the end result to these situations is neither overwhelmingly good nor overwhelmingly bad, so focusing on either is unrealistic.

One man I worked with reached out to me because he was spending hours each week worrying about his son's future. His son had a history of good grades and several hobbies but recently mentioned to his dad that he wanted to leave his sports club. This man found himself asking questions like "Could this be the start of a downward spiral?" and "What if he loses all of his dedication and can't even finish high school?"

When we first started practicing CBT, his response looked like this:

> **R:** I am worrying about my son's choice to stop attending his sports club.
>
> **A:** This is because, if he stops, he might not be able to get into the university he wants and will end up flunking out.
>
> **A:** Am I catastrophizing? Am I giving too much weight to this scenario and not enough to other ones? Is there a chance he could drop this club without sacrificing his chances of getting into universities? Is there a more reasonable middle ground?
>
> **C:** If I look back at my son's history, the worst-case scenario never came true. Even though he has had better and worse years in school, he has still turned out alright. It might help to remember those "good but not great" and "bad but not horrible" years whenever the urge to catastrophize comes up. This will help me assign less value to my son staying in his club, so I will worry about it less.

Like this man did, it is important for us to remind ourselves of the in-betweens. Not only do they make us worry less, they keep us closer to reality.

Jumping to Conclusions

Jumping to conclusions means assuming something is true without clear evidence. This can mean assuming our coworkers are making fun of us for something we did without seeing or hearing them doing it. Or it can mean assuming our significant other is cheating on us based on a hunch.

Jumping to conclusions is harmful because, when we make just one false assumption, it throws off the rest of our logic—when one decision is based on something false, so will all of the others that follow.

We can explore this through the example of one of my colleagues, who approached me because she was spending a lot of time worrying about her relationship with a friend. Specifically, she found herself homing in on his tone of voice—if she felt he was not happy, she assumed he was sad and that it was her fault. This not only led to anxious symptoms but also caused a decrease in her overall mood.

She and I tackled this problem by looking at one of her hangout sessions with him and the conclusions she drew. She said the following:

> **R**: I am worrying that my friend does not want to be friends with me anymore.
>
> **A**: This is because whenever we have hung out recently, I cause him to be less enthusiastic and less talkative.
>
> **A**: Am I jumping to any conclusions here? Is it possible I'm not the reason he is acting this way? Could he be happy to see me even though his tone of voice does not reflect it?
>
> **C**: Not only is that possible, it is probable. He initiates most of our conversations and always asks me to hang out. This shows there is no need to try to make assumptions about our relationship. Next time I have the urge to value his facial expressions and tone of voice, I can counter it with this thought.

As this woman noted, rather than changing our conclusion, it is also okay not to draw one at all, especially when it comes to relationships with others. As humans, our valuations are so different that what we feel is important, like facial expressions for this woman, can be nothing more than an afterthought for others. In her case, as in most cases, the best conclusion we can come to is no conclusion.

Filtering

Filtering, sometimes known as discounting the positive, means valuing only negative experiences and ignoring positive ones. Most commonly, we filter out our positive experiences but not others', leading us to feel overly negative about ourselves—the more positive experiences we ignore, the more negative we will feel.

My example comes from a coworker who approached me when she was worrying about not measuring up. She spent hours browsing social media in her free time, and each time she did, she found herself comparing her own failures to other people's successes.

Her application of CBT looked like this:

R: I am worrying that I am falling behind everyone else.

A: The reason is that, as I see on Instagram, everyone has their life together and I do not. Every time I log on, I see someone hitting a major life goal, but I have not done that in years.

A: Am I filtering out my own positive experiences or their negative ones? Is it possible between all of their accomplishments, they also have negative experiences like I do? Am I comparing one of my low points to one of their high points?

C: Maybe it took those people months or years of improvement to get to where they are. If I look back at their past, I might see them working on themselves, just like I am. It is okay for me not to hit any major milestones right now—that will come in time. Next time I feel the urge to overvalue my negative experiences and undervalue my positive ones, I can remember this.

It is particularly important to understand filtering because certain parts of our lives are already filtered before they reach us. Pictures posted on social media filter the actual story behind them—they show only the best moments of people's lives without showing the hours of boredom or awkwardness in between. News is filtered through the spin each journalist puts on their reports—they regularly play up the points that support their narrative and play down the ones that do not. In fact, just by choosing what news to report and what news to ignore, they filter information. Even the way we humans act in public involves a kind of filtering—especially in the United States, when we socialize, we filter out our negative feelings so that we do not affect those around us. If we want our valuations to be as realistic as possible, we have to be aware of these filters before we draw any conclusions.

On a final note, I discuss use of the internet in the lifestyle changes section.

Overgeneralization

Overgeneralization means assuming one event is part of a larger trend, when it is not—sometimes known as making a mountain out of a molehill. The temptation to overgeneralize is especially common when we have a setback in our recovery; after several weeks or months of behaving healthily, we sometimes fall back into unhealthy habits, leading uncomfortable symptoms to come back for a few days or weeks. These are always temporary and short compared to the rest of our recovery (as I discuss in the recovery roadmap section), but many of us mistakenly take it as a sign we are losing all of our progress.

One young man approached me worrying about a setback he was experiencing. He had been practicing MBCT for weeks and had seen consistent improvement, but one night, he found himself unable to answer suggestive thoughts about sleep, which he thought he had overcome. As some of his old symptoms came back, he spent more and more time worrying that the weeks of progress he made would be canceled out by these few days of discomfort.

The way he tackled this line of thinking was as follows:

R: I am worrying that the return of these symptoms means I am losing all the progress I made.

A: The reason is that these symptoms coming back means I'm in a downward spiral.

A: Am I overgeneralizing? Is it possible to have a few days of anxious symptoms without it being part of a larger trend? Is it possible for me to have this small hiccup without falling back into all of my old habits?

C: If I look back at my last month, I have been making progress almost nonstop. These last four days may have been uncomfortable, but they do not cancel out the month of practice I got with MBCT. In fact, now that I have all that practice, I can dig myself out of this hole even quicker than I did before.

Much like jumping to conclusions, sometimes the best generalization we can make is no generalization at all. On this subject, Shoma Morita, a late-19th, early-20th-century Japanese psychologist, said generalizing is a kind of over-intellectualization—like forcing a grander meaning on something that is meaningless. According to his work, most of our experiences are not part of some trend, and trying to prescribe this kind of meaning to simple situations leads us to needlessly overthink.

If you are in the middle of a setback and would like some more help, I offer a broader discussion on setbacks in the recovery roadmap chapter.

Forest-for-the-Trees Fallacy

The forest-for-the-trees fallacy is the false assumption that we have to consider every detail in a situation when we make a decision rather than focusing on the main factor. This fallacy is problematic because it causes us to assign equal value to every factor in a situation, when realistically most factors have such a small value that they can be ignored. This causes us to spend more time focusing on small details and less time focusing on the most important factor—an unrealistic and inefficient strategy.

This problem has become especially common in the realm of health science, which has been homing in on small factors that affect weight, even though we have had a solid understanding of weight loss science for decades. This has led to hundreds of new diets, supplements, and therapies that focus on minor factors but ultimately fail to produce results.

Here, a family friend approached me because she was worrying about her weight. She had wanted to diet for a long time, but she had been told her metabolism, genetics, muscle composition, stomach bacteria, and sensitivity to certain foods meant she had to craft a diet specifically for her. She knew the number of calories she consumed and burned was the biggest factor, but the worrying she did about the other factors prevented her from ever starting to diet.

Her CBT answer looked like the following:

> **R:** I am worrying that I will be stuck with my weight problems forever.
>
> **A:** The reason is that weight is such a complex issue. I have to consider all of these different things before I even start to diet.
>
> **A:** Am I not seeing the forest for the trees? Is it possible all of these factors are minor? Can I assign more value to one factor over the others and just focus on that?
>
> **C:** It looks like how many calories I eat is the most important for my weight. I will assign the most value to that so I focus most of my attention on it.

As more and more information becomes available to us—not just in the realm of health—understanding this fallacy is vital. The best way to tackle our problems, regardless of what they are about, will be to look at the biggest factor and work outward.

In the context of worrying and anxious symptoms, our mental behavior will always be the biggest factor in our overall health. This means that, for the best results, most of our attention should be focused on changing our behavior through MBCT and CBT, and all other considerations should be secondary.

Personalization

Personalization is the idea that we are entirely to blame for how others feel, or that others are entirely to blame for how we feel. Having valuations based on personalization makes us worry in social situations because, if we think we are responsible for other people's emotions, we will waste a lot of time thinking about them.

One young man approached me about a presentation he had coming up. In the days leading up to the presentation, he spent hours asking himself whether he would screw it up and what it would mean for his relationship with his coworkers.

He used CBT in the following way:

> **R:** I am worrying about screwing up my presentation.
> **A:** The reason is if I do poorly, my coworkers will never be able to look at me the same again.
> **A:** Am I overly personalizing this situation? Could I be way overvaluing my performance on this, even though it might not be a big deal to my coworkers?
> **C:** I know I would not judge them for it, so they probably will not judge me. Maybe, even if I make a mistake, they'll forgive me, so I can value my performance less.

One helpful exercise we can use when we are tempted to personalize is to imagine ourselves in other people's shoes. We do not hastily judge others or focus on the small mistakes they make, so we can assume they will not do it to us, either.

Emotional Reasoning and Having to Worry

Emotional reasoning is defined as using our emotions to justify our actions. For example, using our happiness as a reason to overeat, our sadness as a reason not to do our homework, our anger as a reason to yell at our friends, or our anxious symptoms as a reason to stay home.

Thinking in this way is illogical because, like anxious symptoms, emotions come and go out of our control, often unrelated to our situation; we can feel angry because we are catastrophizing, because we are tired, or because we are hungry. The fact that our emotions do not happen for a logical reason means any actions we base on them will be illogical.

The example I have is of a man who came to me because he felt he could not stop worrying. He worried excessively throughout his life until he became so used to it that *not* worrying felt uncomfortable—choosing to shut down urges like *Should I be worrying?* produced enough adrenaline to make his stomach tighten. He began to believe his discomfort meant he was stuck worrying for life, a thought that made him pessimistic about recovering.

Our discussion about this looked like the following:

> **R:** I am worrying right now.
> **A:** I am worrying because I have to! It feels weird if I do not.
> **A:** Am I using emotional reasoning, overvaluing my discomfort? Is it possible I can choose not to worry and allow this discomfort, knowing it will benefit me?

C: I now know how to respond to this urge to worry, so I will give this a shot to see if it causes me to worry less.

If what this man experienced resonates with you, I have a discussion about what the long-term recovery process looks like later on.

Note that acting despite our feelings and emotions is not the same as not allowing them. Like with anxious symptoms, the key is to let happiness, sadness, emptiness, anger, and discomfort manifest as they want, but choose to act logically and realistically regardless.

Control Fallacy

The control fallacy has two meanings. The first is when we try to control something that we physically cannot, leading us to waste a lot of time and effort without producing any results. For example, we may try to control anxious symptoms through deep breathing, leading us to spend needless hours worrying that gets us nowhere.

The second is assuming something is out of our control, when really it is not. For example, when we have been worrying for many years and trying to stop is uncomfortable, some of us falsely assume we cannot change our behavior.

One woman who approached me had this attitude toward her worrying: she worried that, no matter what she did, she would be stuck worrying forever. She addressed this line of thinking as follows:

R: I am worrying that I cannot stop worrying.

A: Why? Because my worrying just isn't in my control.

A: Could this be the control fallacy? Am I undervaluing my ability to act in a different way? Some of the factors may be out of my control, but is there anything I can change?

C: Maybe the factor that is out of my control right now is my discomfort with not worrying. This means it will be incredibly difficult to stop worrying all at once. However, I can definitely take small steps toward worrying less. This is the part that is in my control.

The control fallacy illustrates why it is so important to understand the biology behind worrying and anxious symptoms. Once we understand our anxious symptoms are out of our conscious control, we stop wasting time trying to control them. Once we understand the ways we can change our behavior, we become able to reduce how much we worry.

Should Statements

The should-statement fallacy is defined as overusing the word "should" when we set expectations for ourselves. Examples include "I should be working" or "I should be on a diet."

The problem with using should statements is that they are subjective; what a person feels they should be doing differs based on culture, religion, family, and education level. In other words, there are no objective shoulds.

Even if our valuations are logical, using the word "should" puts unnecessary pressure on us. When we are not doing what we should be doing, we feel like we are wasting time, leading us to feel guilty. And when we finally do what we should have been doing, it will feel long overdue, draining the satisfaction we could be getting.

One man approached me, worrying right before he graduated from university. He had just landed his dream job and all of his friends and family were cheering him on. However, he was in a period of high adrenaline and experiencing uncomfortable anxious symptoms. Although he felt he should be excited, he was not because of his physical condition, and this led him to feel guilty.

The discussion we had resulted in the following application of CBT:

R: I am worrying about not being excited for my new job.

A: This is because I should be excited. It is my dream job, after all.

A: Is it possible I am using an unnecessary should statement? Could this statement be putting undue pressure on me and making me feel worse?

C: I can abandon this should statement. I know why my body is reacting this way, and saying I should feel differently is not only unhelpful, it is false.

Coming to this conclusion can be difficult, especially if we have been using should statements for many years. For this reason, CBT practitioner David Burns says we can subtly change them rather than let them go completely. His suggestion is to replace the phrase "I should" with "It would be beneficial for me if..." This puts less pressure on us and gives us a chance to feel satisfaction when we act.

Fairness Fallacy

The fairness fallacy is defined as the idea that the world should be fair, that all humans should be repaid for the good things they do and punished for the bad. The fairness fallacy fails for the same reason should statements do: fairness is subjective and varies all around the world.

Fairness feels like such a big issue when we experience anxious symptoms because there are so many people out there who do not. And when these symptoms have such a negative impact on our lives, many of us start to believe we have been robbed of something.

The issue with focusing on fairness is that we cannot compare our problems to others. There are many of us who have panic attacks but have never experienced depressive symptoms. Some of us have experienced both but have never lost a loved one. The range of problems we can go through in life is so large that it is impossible to establish what is truly fair.

The other issue with focusing on fairness is that it keeps us focused on the past rather than the present. As you now know, anxious symptoms are infinitely treatable when we change our behavior, so giving too much attention to how uncomfortable we *used* to be means we will focus less on how comfortable we *can* be.

To illustrate this, I would like to share the case of a young woman who was worrying about her boyfriend's anxious symptoms. His issues began when he was young, and by the time he sought help, his adrenaline levels were high enough to cause daily episodes of nausea. She worried about this because she thought his case was especially bad and spent more time thinking about who to blame than how to help her boyfriend.

She approached her thinking as follows:

> **R:** I am worrying that my boyfriend is struggling with anxious symptoms.
>
> **A:** Why? Because it is not fair. If we could find someone else who was responsible for this, maybe they could fix it.
>
> **A:** Is this the fairness fallacy? Is it possible that focusing on fairness is not important right now? Are there better ways to help my boyfriend?
>
> **C:** Maybe encouraging him to stick to treatment will go a lot further than looking for who to blame. If I value the idea of fairness less, I will spend less time thinking about it.

There will be times in which fairness is a legitimate issue in our lives—in which there is an actual problem that is best fixed by the person who caused it. However, the best time to handle actual issues of fairness is after we have fully recovered, so we can go in with a clear head and devote the proper attention to it.

Labeling

Labeling is defining ourselves or others using words that make us feel guilty and restrict our behavior. For example, we may label ourselves stupid. This is problematic because we will give ourselves fewer chances to do things that are for "smart people," like going to lectures and reading books. On the other hand, if we label ourselves smart, we will feel bad when we do things we do not consider smart, like drop an AP class or do poorly on a test.

The reason labeling is unhelpful is that, much like many of these other distortions, labels are subjective and overly simplistic. What may seem smart to one person will seem stupid to another. Many of us feel we are smart in our hobbies but stupid in our work, or smart in theory but practically stupid, even when others disagree. Labeling ourselves in this way is not only unrealistic, it holds us back without giving us any benefit.

One young man asked for my help because he was worrying about his progress as a musician. He had always been a talented guitar player, ever since he was young, and after being called a gifted student in guitar for many years, he stuck the label on himself.

However, he reached a point where his lack of knowledge of music theory was holding him back, and to get better, he had to pick up his first ever music theory book. Yet, whenever he thought about doing so, he worried that he would not be able to understand it, and so he put it off for months. His CBT response looked like this:

> **R:** I am worrying about learning music theory.
> **A:** This is because if I do not do well, I will find out I am not really a gifted student.

A: Is it possible that, by labeling myself, I am giving too much weight to fitting this label? If I stopped thinking of myself in these terms, would I be okay with not understanding music theory on the first pass?

C: I will try ditching this label and reading through the book without expectations for myself. Even if I do not understand it perfectly the first time, it will not matter, so I might as well try.

It is important to note that dropping a label is not the same as dropping all the values within it; we can stop labeling ourselves as gifted students and still value academics, or stop labeling ourselves as musicians and still value music. Dropping the label only leaves us more open to act differently when we need to.

Besides academics, some areas where we commonly label ourselves are work, race or ethnicity, religion, sexuality, and gender, though the list is not limited to these topics. The fewer labels we give ourselves, the freer we will be to try things that could benefit us.

Always Being Right

In CBT, always being right means focusing more on proving ourselves right than on the truth. For example, we might say to ourselves that we are going to have anxious symptoms forever, which will lead us to spend more time looking at people who fit this description and less time looking at people who have recovered. This is problematic because, when we value our opinion over the truth, we will avoid acting in ways that prove we are wrong, even if they might help us.

Most often, we overvalue being right when we think there is pressure on us. One young mother approached me worrying about her son's problems with anxious symptoms. Her son had recently hit a period of high adrenaline and was experiencing nausea strong enough to prevent him from eating. She had never been taught about how adrenaline affects the body, so in her mind, this nausea was only in his imagination. As a result, she spent a lot of time on the internet looking for parents with similar opinions and avoiding websites that discussed how to actually handle the issue.

She applied CBT as follows:

> **R:** I'm worrying about my son.
> **A:** I'm worrying because he is making a big deal out of symptoms that are all in his head.
> **A:** Is it possible I am prioritizing being right over my son's health? Is there a possibility these symptoms actually are real?
> **C:** That may be the case. If I at least treat them this way, maybe it will help me understand what he is going through.

Here, the CBT method helps us not only figure out where we are wrong but also why we feel the need to be right. In this woman's case, admitting she was wrong would mean confronting a difficult situation—having to see her son through treatment, a long and uncomfortable process. But by exploring this, she eventually made the change that led her son to recover.

Meaningful Suffering (Heaven's Reward)

The heaven's-reward or meaningful-suffering fallacy is the mistaken idea that discomfort—like illness or pain—will always lead to benefit in the long run. Though this fallacy has religious origins, none of the Semitic religions actually preach this idea. The problem with this mentality is that suffering is *not* inherently meaningful; when we fall seriously ill, get our money stolen, or lose a loved one, it does not pay off and only hurts us.

Sometimes, when we effectively plan out and monitor certain activities that make us suffer, like certain exercises, certain diets, and certain therapies, they can bring rewards. But while suffering is a part of improving, it is not the *reason* we improve. In fact, when we go about exercising, dieting, and therapy in an unscientific way, we can suffer without ever improving.

One man approached me worrying about his health. He wanted to stop worrying, but was concerned that, if he did, it would come at the cost of getting terminally ill without catching it in time. In other words, as uncomfortable as worrying made him, he thought that it brought benefits.

Our discussion looked like the following:

> **R:** I am worrying about not worrying.
>
> **A:** The reason is that if I stop worrying, I may get sick and fall ill without catching it in time.
>
> **A:** Is this the meaningful-suffering fallacy? Am I giving too much value to worrying? Is it possible I can still recognize when I am feeling uncomfortable and go to the doctor but not worry about it afterward?
>
> **C:** This is what my friends and family do, and they have been able to take care of their health well enough. Maybe I can too.

This distortion is why I wanted to review the most common anxious symptoms in the MBCT chapter—when we know which symptoms are a harmless side effect of adrenaline and which ones require further investigation, it makes us much less likely to fall into the trap of excessively worrying about our health.

EXPOSURE AND RESPONSE PREVENTION

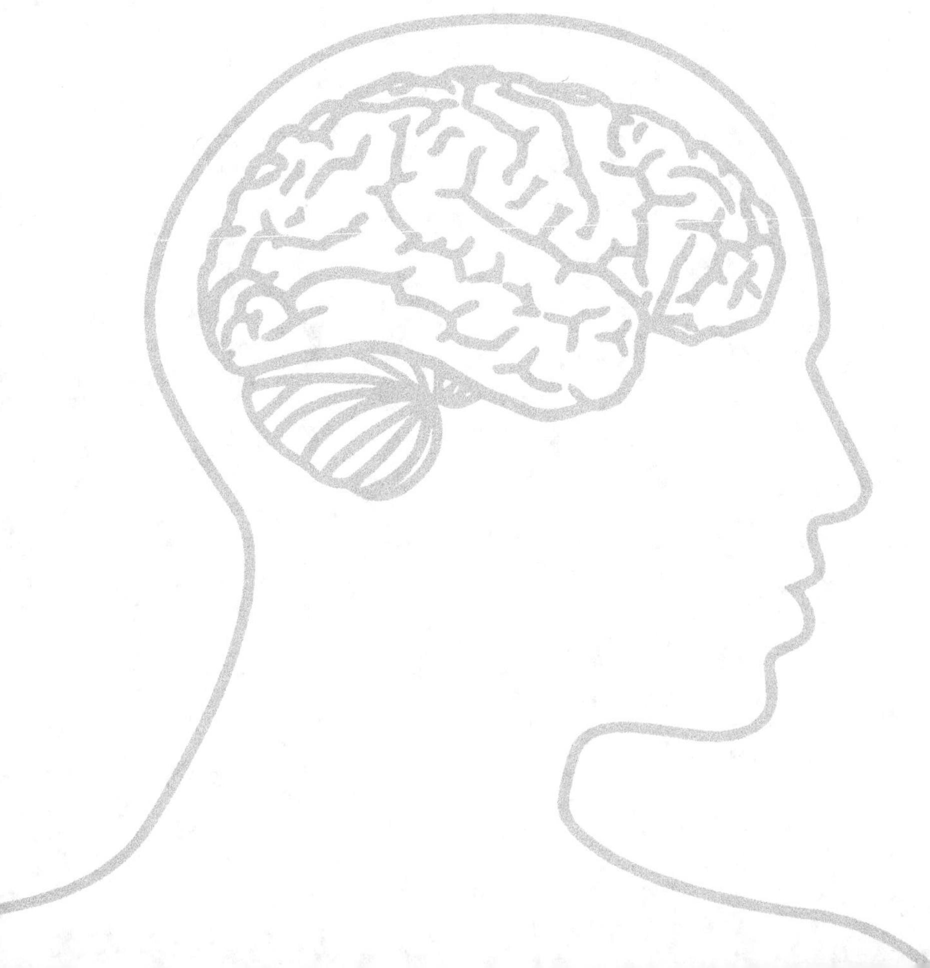

The ERP Method to Reduce the Strength of Anxious Symptoms

Exposure and response prevention is the last form of therapy I will discuss in this book. The previous two therapies, MBCT and CBT, were used to change our conscious cortex. This chapter will focus only on the amygdala's internal programming—a much smaller (though still important) part of the recovery process.

Theory: The Fight or Flight Response

Recalling from the first chapter, there are two reasons our amygdala produces adrenaline. The first is when we worry—worrying causes our conscious cortex to activate the amygdala, leading anxious symptoms to go on for as long as we keep worrying. The second reason is the amygdala activating itself, due to its own internal programming. When this happens, the amygdala has safeguards in place to prevent it from self-activating for too long, so if we do not worry, the adrenaline rush will not last for more than a few minutes.

You also read that the amygdala changes based on experience—experiences that end in discomfort cause it to dial up its response, while those that end comfortably cause it to dial it down. If we feel our amygdala's response is too strong and want to weaken it, we can expose it to more positive experiences.[16]

That is the purpose of ERP: To schedule sessions in which we **e**xpose our amygdala to a stressor that activates it, then **p**revent ourselves from engaging in a negative **r**esponse so that our amygdala can desensitize.

We have already reviewed the response portion—MBCT and CBT—so this chapter will only focus on exposure.

ERP Method: Rules of ERP

Exposure methods in ERP follow four rules:[16]

1. To change the amygdala, we need to apply stress to it. Practically, this means we have to expose ourselves to a stressor for longer than we are used to (at least ten or fifteen minutes after the most powerful waves of adrenaline have passed) before we choose to end the exposure session.

2. To avoid giving ourselves too much work in the response portion, we should start small.

3. To make our amygdala retain these experiences, we have to keep exposing ourselves constantly and over time.

4. To be as productive as possible, we should gradually increase our exposure to the stressor. The more we expose ourselves, the more comfortable we will get with a stressor—and the less stress it will apply to our amygdala. If we want to keep progressing, we need to practice **progressive overload**, increasing the frequency, time, or volume of exposure as we get more comfortable.

For this, there are three ERP methods that we can use, depending on the nature of our stressor and how directly we want to confront it.

Applied ERP: Direct, Indirect, and Imaginal

Direct ERP

The simplest way we can expose our amygdala to its stressors is directly. This method is most effective for stressors that are easily accessible and works best after we have plenty of experience practicing MBCT so we do not worry.

For those of us who experience anxious symptoms at school, direct ERP means attending class and letting all of our worst symptoms manifest while using MBCT to stop ourselves from worrying. For those of us who avoid socializing at work, this means sitting in the break room or regularly attending work functions and using MBCT to prevent panic.

After a few direct ERP sessions, our amygdala's response begins to weaken,[74] so we have to up the intensity of frequency of our exposure. If attending class no longer produces symptoms, but they still come up when speaking with others, we should make some light small talk once a day to further desensitize. If we get comfortable with small talk, we should try for extended conversations. With enough time, anxious symptoms will hardly come up at all, even in these more pressing situations.

Indirect ERP

The second form of ERP is indirect ERP—exposure to a similar but less intense situation. Indirect ERP is most useful for stressors that are too infrequent to practice directly—infrequent physical situations like flying or infrequent social ones like biannual group presentations.

In indirect ERP, the goal is to identify what sensation in our actual stressor causes our amygdala to activate, then simulate these sensations in an activity that is more accessible. For example, many people who experience symptoms on a plane ride have trouble with takeoff and landing. One way we can simulate this feeling without paying thousands of dollars for practice flights is by riding elevators. Once we have a good handle on elevator rides, we might graduate to more intense situations, like roller coasters. For infrequent social situations, there are organizations that can simulate different activities, like interview practice organizations and public speaking groups.

We can also use indirect ERP as a lead-in to direct ERP if we do not yet feel comfortable with direct confrontation. For example, we can have mock interviews with our therapist or role-play with friends in preparation for a job interview. Once we become comfortable with indirect ERP, we must progressively overload our amygdala by directly confronting the stressor.

Imaginal ERP

Sometimes, our amygdala will not be sensitive to physical situations, but it will activate when we experience a certain suggestive thought. One example is if our amygdala creates a burst of adrenaline whenever we have a thought of going crazy or dying. There is nothing we can do to simulate actually going crazy or dying, so the only way we can expose ourselves is by imagining what it would be like, also known as imaginal ERP.

Most often, imaginal ERP is done through role-play with a talk therapist. In an imaginal ERP session, our therapist gives us a thought that activates our amygdala and we imagine how we would act. An example of this might be "Imagine you are going crazy. What is happening?"

Then we play out this scenario in words, using MBCT and CBT every time we are tempted to worry.

This kind of role-play can also be used to address situations that we do not yet feel comfortable confronting, even indirectly, like riding in an elevator or going to a meeting. Imagining the situation can be used to decrease our amygdala's response so that after a few sessions, we can transition into indirect ERP more easily.

Another reason we might use ERP is if our amygdala activates when we get a suggestive thought about a memory—sometimes called memorial ERP.

The practice behind memorial ERP is the same: our therapist reminds us of a painful memory and asks us to sit with the uncomfortable symptoms, using MBCT and CBT to refrain from worrying.

I personally used to experience great pain whenever I was reminded of my worst moments with anxious symptoms: days without more than a few minutes of sleep, weeks without being able to eat or drink, and months of constant intrusive thoughts and other anxious symptoms. Every time these suggestive thoughts popped up, I would get a burst of adrenaline, making the experience even more uncomfortable. Memorial ERP was the way I finally broke free of these memories. I revisited them every week with my therapist, examining why I worried about them and responding with MBCT. The more I healthily exposed myself, the less adrenaline these memories brought up, until I could relive them without experiencing any discomfort.

LIFESTYLE CHANGES

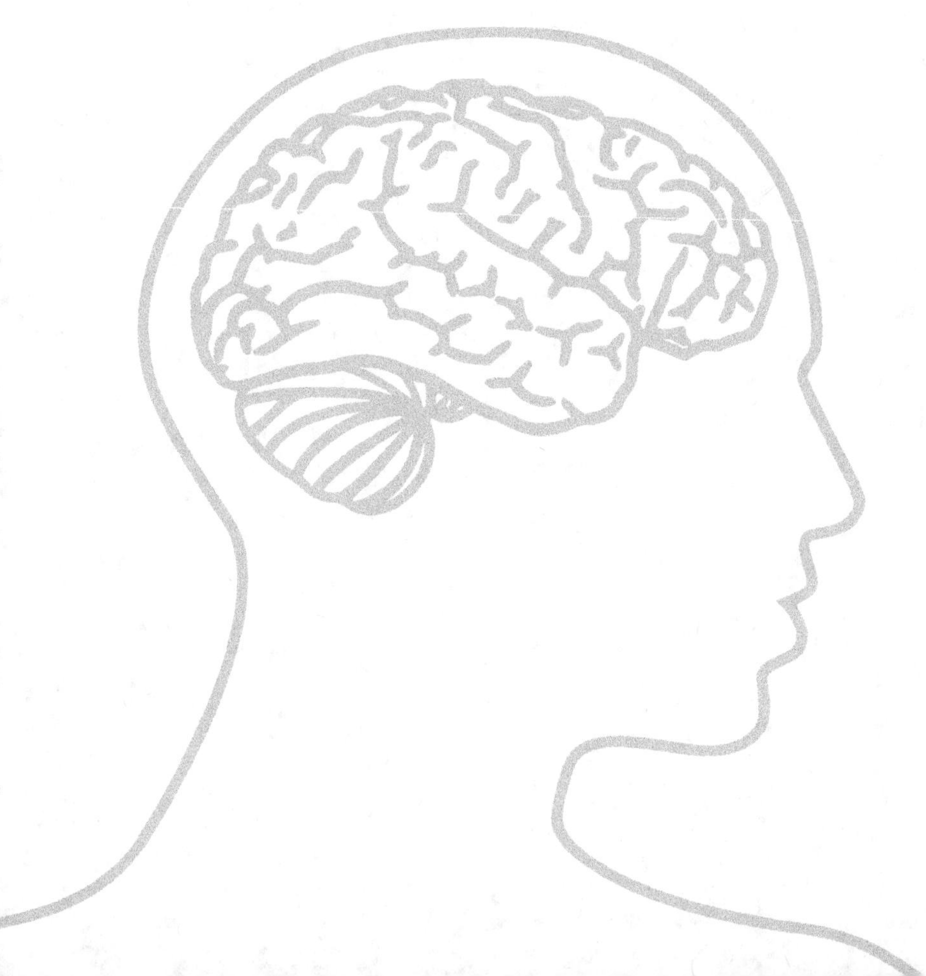

Lifestyle Changes to Accelerate Your Recovery

The therapy techniques discussed in this book will be the key to recovery and should be your focus. However, you may benefit from trying a few of the following recommendations to help you practice them more effectively, as well as to reduce discomfort in the interim.

Exercise Often

Everyone has heard about the benefits of exercise. Doing so three to five times a week for a period of a half hour or more boosts our mood, gives us a chance to have fun, and helps with overall health. We become more energy-efficient, age more slowly, and become less susceptible to illness.[75]

In addition, when we set goals for ourselves, exercise becomes an especially good return activity; when we want to stay focused on running for longer or lifting heavier weights, it makes the urge to worry feel that much weaker.

It is also important to think of how *not* exercising impacts us during a period of high adrenaline. As we discussed in the biology section, our body is constantly making and trying to get rid of adrenaline. If we do not use it, our body has to let it out through anxious symptoms. The less we use, the more symptoms our body produces. By exercising, we give our body a chance to use adrenaline productively rather than just sit through the discomfort.

The only caveat to this is that, during exercise, our heart rate rises and our breathing becomes quick, so if we are tempted to worry about this, we can use MBCT.

Whatever exercise we choose should be simple and easy for the first week or two—half-hour runs and empty barbells or free weights. Then, we should practice progressive overload, gradually increasing the intensity, weight, or frequency.

Maintain These Aspects of your Diet

When it comes to diet, there are three factors that impact anxious symptoms: water, electrolytes, and caffeine.

As discussed earlier, the body needs a certain balance of electrolytes and water to function. If our organs do not have enough water or salts, our body has to deliver more blood to them to compensate. It does so by constricting our blood vessels, which causes the heart and lungs to go into overdrive.[76] Though this biological process is different from adrenaline, there is some overlap in the symptoms. For this reason, if we want to minimize the amount of time we spend with uncomfortable symptoms, we should drink water whenever we start to feel thirsty and make sure to get enough salts in our diet. Even if we feel too nauseated to eat, this means we should have an electrolyte candy and drink water every once in a while.

It also means we must avoid substances that dehydrate us. The two most common ones are caffeine and alcohol. Both of these are diuretics, which means they make us urinate more. This leads our body to release water and electrolytes more quickly and increases the chance we will experience anxious symptoms.

Caffeine has the added problem of causing our blood vessels to constrict, even when we are properly hydrated. It does so by binding to the adenosine receptors in the brain, which are partially responsible for blood flow. If we already have a high level of adrenaline, caffeine can amplify the strength of our symptoms.[77]

When our baseline level of adrenaline is low and we can respond to anxious symptoms easily, we can return to drinking coffee and alcohol. But during the recovery period, it is best to stay away.

Meditate the Right Way

Just like exercise, meditation is proven to have positive effects on all kinds of bodily processes, from mood to digestion.[78] And as something we can do at home and even in bed, there is no reason not to.

However, before we start to meditate, it is important to understand how to do it. In movies and TV shows, characters are shown meditating by "clearing" their mind and sitting in silence, then coming out feeling refreshed. As any experienced meditator can tell you, it is impossible to make our brain stop thinking like that, and actual meditation is physically and mentally draining.

This unrealistic understanding of meditation is why so many people struggle to get into it. If our goal is to fight against the thoughts our brain makes for a half hour, then pretend like we enjoyed it, we will not last a week. For us to actually benefit from meditation, we have to work with the brain rather than against it.

As you know, our emotional brain is constantly producing suggestive thoughts out of our conscious control. Thus, the focus should be to shut down the urge to consider them and return our attention to something else. If this sounds familiar, that is because you have already done it in MBCT; meditation is just a way to practice MBCT in a vacuum, with our eyes closed, sitting in a sustainable posture, in a comfortable atmosphere.

Our meditation routine should look something like this: First, we choose a length of time to meditate and set a timer. Second, we get seated or lie down in a comfortable position that we can hold and that keeps our airways open. This might be sitting on a blanket with our legs crossed, straight up on an armchair, or lying down on a yoga mat. Third, we pick something to focus on for our return step. Most often, people choose something rhythmic that they can count like their breathing, or a pleasant image like clouds passing over a mountain. What we choose is not particularly important as long as it draws our focus. Then we begin focusing on it.

After a few seconds of focusing, suggestive thoughts will begin to pop up. We can simply ignore the smaller ones and return to our image. If we notice ourselves starting to consider one, we can respond to that urge the way we do in MBCT and return to again.

After a few minutes, we begin to get tired of responding and notice ourselves considering suggestive thoughts for longer and longer. When this happens, we should try our best to keep responding, but if we cannot, it is okay. Once our time is up, we put everything back and return to our day.

If we have not been responding to suggestive thoughts for our whole lives, our brain will have to restructure itself to get used to meditative behavior. This means meditating will be difficult at first. But the more often we meditate, the easier it will be and the longer we will be able to do it.

For those first starting out, I recommend meditating for five minutes twice a day, adding a minute or two every few days.

Practice Realistic Visualization

Visualization can be a powerful desensitizing tool. When we imagine ourselves succeeding in a situation, it can work like imaginal ERP, making our amygdala less sensitive to it. However, like meditation, there have been so many misconceptions about visualization that most people do it incorrectly.

Most visualization exercises have us imagining ourselves succeeding more than we ever thought possible. If we are running a race, we visualize ourselves reaching the finish line with a big smile, surrounded by friends and family, minutes before our goal time. For presentations, we visualize our audience engaged the whole time and our explanations going off without a hitch.

The problem with using visualization in this way is that it creates unrealistic expectations, which as you read earlier, does more harm than good—it sets the bar so high that anything less will feel like a disappointment. This is especially true when we are going through a period of high adrenaline, as trying to imagine *any* situation without anxious symptoms feels worthless.

Even in my best races, I finished sweaty and beat-up without anyone waiting for me at the finish, sometimes missing my goal pace by five minutes. In my best presentations, I stuttered, had a few awkward silences, and was hit with questions I did not expect. I also have yet to come across an audience that is so engaged that they spend the whole time on the edge of their seats.

Realistically, during these events, we will not feel especially good or especially bad. Our performance will be average, and our audience will be okay at best.

For visualization to actually feel meaningful, we have to take these things into account and use a more realistic approach: rather than visualizing ourselves having giant success, we should imagine ourselves just passing—imagining ourselves experiencing all the uncomfortable thoughts and symptoms we are used to but being able to deal with them like we always have.

A few of those I have worked with have used visualization for presentations at school and at work. When I spoke with them, they visualized getting to their presentation with their heart rate already high. They visualized thoughts of going crazy popping up in the moments before they started speaking and then throughout the presentation. They visualized not being able to answer some of the questions they received. But most importantly, they visualized themselves making it through.

Once they finished the speech and things went as expected, it boosted their confidence in their ability to make it through difficult situations and prepared them to do it again.

Maintain Proper Sleep Hygiene

While sleeping well might not do much to reduce daytime anxious symptoms, sleeping poorly can certainly increase them. When we do not get proper sleep, our body has to work harder during the day. To do this, it constricts our blood vessels,[79] which as you know, can cause anxious symptoms. In addition, the grogginess we feel when we do not sleep well can make it more difficult to focus on MBCT and CBT.

I covered the use of MBCT for insomnia and anxious symptoms earlier, but there is one more factor that impacts our sleep: light exposure. Our body produces sleep-inducing hormones most efficiently in the dark and waking hormones in the light.[80] If we want to go to sleep more quickly and sleep for longer, we should have as little light exposure as possible.

This means we should turn off bright screens as we get ready for bed. It also means, when we wake up in the middle of the night, we should not turn on any lights, phones, or computers.

For this, I recommend a sleep mask. It takes a few nights to get used to, but it functions like blackout curtains for your eyes—minimizing light exposure and allowing you to have more consistent sleep.

Take Break Days

While we should spend as much time as we can on exposure exercises, sometimes we feel tired and do not want to. In fact, everyone has these limits, even those who have no problems with anxious symptoms. When this happens, we can benefit from taking a break.

Breaks are important because they give our brain time to parse what we learned in the last week without interruption, so they are necessary, even when we do not enjoy them. This may mean taking one day each week to allow ourselves to stay home and play games rather than leave the house, or take a long bath and eat our favorite foods alone rather than engage socially. As our condition improves, these days will become more enjoyable, and we will need them less frequently. Still, even those who have fully recovered may benefit from taking one day a month to destress.

Speak to a Therapist

Therapists are like dieticians or fitness instructors—they are there to help us establish healthy habits and, as we get used to them, to check and correct our methods. They are not necessary for making progress, but they can be helpful in pointing out our cognitive blind spots.

The ideal talk therapy session, like the ideal training session, is composed of the following: a review of what we achieved in the last week, a practice of the techniques we will be using this week (such as in CBT or ERP), a discussion of any hangups we might have, and a time to plan for the week ahead.

The experience we have in therapy will depend a lot on which therapist we pick. If we have someone who is knowledgeable and works well with us, we can make a lot of progress. If we do not, however, it can hold us back. For this reason, I have made the following checklist that we can use to find the ideal therapist:

1. Does my therapist have experience with anxious symptoms and excessive worrying?
2. Is my therapist nonjudgmental?

3. Does my therapist listen to me?
4. Do I have good chemistry with my therapist?
5. Does my therapist dispense helpful advice?
6. Does my therapist help me improve in meaningful ways?

The ideal therapist also requires an ideal patient; their guidance will only help as long as we use it. For this reason, I created this checklist we can use to analyze ourselves and make sure we are getting the most out of therapy:

1. What am I trying to get out of therapy?
2. Am I entirely honest with my therapist?
3. Do I accept my therapist's advice nonjudgmentally?
4. Do I allow my therapist to disagree with me?
5. Have I been doing my homework?
6. Have I worked with my therapist for long enough to make decisions about him or her? (My recommendation is at least four sessions with a therapist before deciding to stay or switch)

Have a Healthy Support Network

Having a healthy support network can make a world of difference during recovery. When we have people to share in our successes and help us push past setbacks, it can make our journey a lot smoother. However, not all support networks are born equal, and having no support network can sometimes be better than having a bad one. If we want to maximize our recovery, we should make sure of the following:

Our support network should be a lot like our therapist—nonjudgmental. They should accept us as we are in the moment, just like we accept ourselves.

They should also offer support and comfort us. However, we must be aware of the difference between comforting and enabling. One of the keys to our recovery is exposing ourselves to uncomfortable symptoms, situations, and valuations. While *we* know this, our friends and family may not. This can lead them to mistakenly behave in ways that hold us back—encouraging us to stay home when we feel uncomfortable or encouraging us to keep visiting doctors even after we have tested negative for everything.

If we recognize them behaving this way, it is our responsibility to discuss with them why it is unhelpful and give them a chance to change, reminding them when necessary. If after repeated discussions they keep acting in the same way, we must distance ourselves, at least until we recover; keeping an enabler in the loop for the months we recover is not worth the discomfort we experience as a result. This may mean refusing to discuss certain topics with them, even if we want to, or contacting them less outright.

We must also have realistic expectations for our support network. While friends and family can help us in the beginning, they cannot accompany us every step of the way. If we can apply MBCT and CBT only in the presence of a loved one, it means we still have a lot of work to do. In addition, they have their own lives. If helping us recover prevents them from solving their own problems, it is best for us to take a step back and reconsider our dynamic with them.

This is the approach we should take when supporting others. Helping our loved ones is a great way to maintain our relationship, but if doing so impedes our own recovery, our capacity to keep helping will decrease. The most sustainable way to help others is to do so only when it does not hurt us. Having these expectations for ourselves and others is the best way to ensure a productive support network for everyone.

Ditch Unhealthy Online Habits

The internet has brought us some major benefits in the last twenty years, but it has also enabled some of our worst behaviors. While we are recovering, there are two things we must make sure of:

First, we must not google symptoms. Before starting treatment, I used to spend hours self-diagnosing and watching videos about people with the conditions I thought I had. As you read earlier, this behavior is unproductive because the only people qualified to diagnose and treat us are doctors, and any time we spend googling symptoms keeps us needlessly worrying. The healthiest way to address this, at least until we have recovered, is to stop googling completely—identifying the urge to do it and shutting it down with MBCT.

Second, we must not overuse social media. As we discussed in the CBT chapter, the information that gets posted on social media goes through a filter; the pictures we see do not tell the full story, and the news stories we post are overly negative. If you want to see this for yourself, you can try out this experiment: next time you log on to social media, scroll through your feed and look at the first thirty posts. Count how many of them are focused on worrying, anger, or making us jealous, how many are neutral, and how many are positive. For most of us, the vast majority will be negative or neutral, and the positive ones will only make us feel short-lasting pleasure.[81] Thus the best way to use social media is for directly contacting others and nothing more.

This is especially true of news aggregation sites like Reddit. While these sites welcome all kinds of news, the only articles that float to the top are those that elicit a reaction from us—almost always negative ones. Some of these sites come with anonymous forums where users can discuss specific topics, like anxious symptoms. Such forums were created to help anxious people find help but ironically have the opposite effect; the majority of posts are people worrying about long-term anxious symptoms, and the support and achievement posts are only about short-term highs.

In reality, there are thousands of people recovering from anxious symptoms every day, but when we spend time on these forums, it is easy to miss that fact. On this subject, my therapist once gave me a nugget of wisdom: "We don't go on these sites to find success stories, and even when we do, they don't stick." The best way we can engage with these sites is to look at the resources they have for recovery and to avoid the forums entirely.

Be Optimistic

When most of us have had so many negative experiences with anxious symptoms, it is common for us to be pessimistic toward the future—to believe that most of our lives will be negative and positive experiences will be the exception. However, as more and more studies come out[82] on the subject, we are realizing that not only is optimism the healthier choice, it is also the more realistic one.

We can use ourselves as an example here by thinking back to the last problem we faced. It could be an argument with a loved one or a mistake we made at work. Then, we can analyze the anxious discomfort we felt by asking the following question: *Was the discomfort I experienced due to the problem itself or my worrying about it?*

If we look around us, there are people who argue with loved ones, make mistakes at work, and even go through periods of high adrenaline but only experience negative emotions very briefly. This is not because they experience fewer problems than the average person, nor is it because they are born less negative. Rather, it is because they do not worry about or ruminate on their problems, leading the negative emotions that follow to be much shorter and less intense. As a result, they are able to return to baseline more quickly and stay there for longer. This leads us to an important conclusion: it is not the problems we face in our lives that lead to overwhelming emotional discomfort but rather our behavior in response to them.

If we look at our whole life with this same detached lens, we can see that most of it is non-negative. When we get up in the morning to get a drink and take a shower, our water runs at the temperature we want. When we cook breakfast, our gas works and the food we make does not make us sick. We have clothes to keep us warm and air conditioning to keep us cool. We ride a bike, car, bus, or train to get us to our work, which even on our worst days, we get through without any major issues. Occasionally, we get into an argument, fall ill, hurt ourselves, or lose money, but these incidents happen infrequently. The time they occupy is short, and even as we are fixing them, everything else continues to work as it is supposed to. This is the definition of optimism—understanding that most of our life goes without issue and that negative emotions never last when we react to them properly.

Having this understanding is especially important during our recovery. If we respond to negative experiences with pessimism, we become more likely to worry, and extend the cycle of anxious symptoms. But when we respond positively—knowing that negativity is temporary and we will keep getting better—it becomes much easier to enjoy the small victories and stay realistic.

It is also why so many former pessimists become optimistic when they adopt more logical thinking through CBT;[83] once they cut off behavior that causes these symptoms, the discomfort they experience around problems is much shorter, so sadness and anger become the exception and not the rule.

Many people believe optimism means forcing positivity on every situation, but this is not the case. If we are home with the flu or in a period of grief, the last thing we should do is try to trick ourselves into thinking we are happy. That only denies our body the chance to release negative emotions, leading them to be more drawn out. Optimism actually means understanding that these uncomfortable periods are temporary and short—the exception and not the rule. This mindset makes it easier to allow problems to happen, as they always do, and to take care of them on our own time.

If you are having difficulty making the switch, it is okay. I want you to keep this discussion in mind as you have more and more positive experiences throughout your recovery.

Act Now

To conclude this chapter, I want to discuss when to make a change. So many of us want to do things that will benefit us, like meditate, practice therapies, and exercise, but we wait for the motivation boost to start or put it off until the "perfect time."

The problem with waiting until we feel motivated was actually discussed in the emotional reasoning section: emotions like motivation come and go out of our control, and we cannot rely on them.

In fact, when we look at people who *do* rely on motivation, we see that they have problems sticking to the changes they try to make. The most common example of this is when we make New Year's resolutions. At the start of the new year, we are filled with motivation to achieve long-term goals. Yet only about a tenth of us make it all the way through, despite our motivation.[84]

As we saw in the CBT chapter, the healthiest way to approach motivation is to do what we do with all other emotions: act *regardless* of how we feel. I and so many people I work with have woken up to that invisible force trying to keep us in bed, fighting us every second of the day. But when we stopped treating this feeling like a command, we saw all of the things we could do, even when it was there.

After weeks of acting without motivation, it starts to feel easier. Even when we have no energy, we have enough experience working through it to know we can do it anyway. This makes difficult days less difficult and easier days feel effortless. In my eyes, this is a more realistic definition for motivation: the feeling of remembering the weeks of work we have done toward our goal and the desire to keep that change going, even through emotional low points. By looking at it this way, we will be able to stay motivated even when we are busy, tired, or uncomfortable.

If you have an idea for a change you want to make, now would be a great time to put down this book and do it. Not only will it lead to a clean house, a good meal, or a productive workout, it will be an invaluable investment in your relationship with motivation.

RECOVERY
ROADMAP

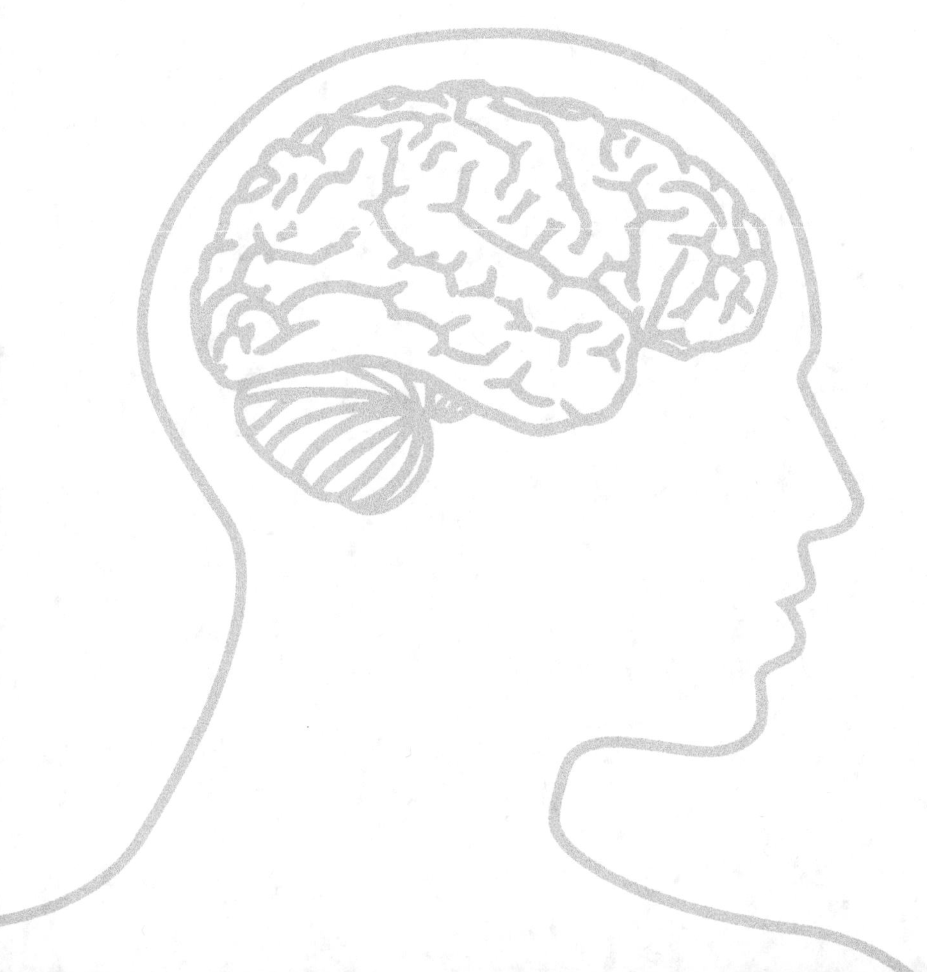

Recovery Roadmap

After starting to recover, it is natural to wonder how long it will take or whether we are on the right track. Now, I want to answer any questions you may have by giving you a general roadmap for your recovery.

As we have discussed, problems with anxious symptoms are rooted in worrying. When we worry, our brain becomes more comfortable with doing so more often. In addition, it leads the amygdala to produce adrenaline, which our body lets out through symptoms. When our adrenaline levels are low, we will only experience mild mental symptoms, like more serious suggestive thoughts more often. But as we continue, our adrenaline levels increase until we experience physical symptoms like nausea, high heart rate, and shortness of breath. The more often we worry, the stronger and more frequent these symptoms will get, until they show up all day, every day.

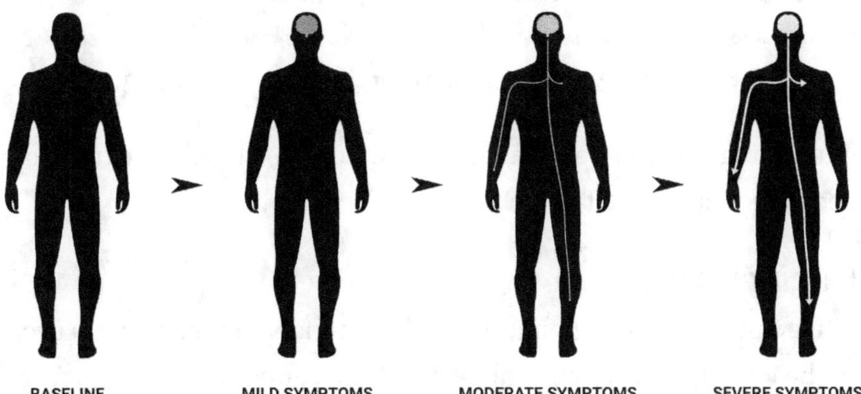

The progression of adrenaline and the anxious symptoms it causes.

Looking at this progression, we can say that anxious symptoms begin in the brain and work their way outward to the heart, lungs, stomach, and muscles as they get more intense.

Recovery looks like this in reverse. When we curb our worrying, it leads our body to make less adrenaline, causing physical symptoms like nausea and shaking to become weaker. Eventually, they become so weak that they are unnoticeable, leaving us with only mental symptoms. As we worry less and expose our amygdala to more of its stressors, our body dials down its adrenaline even more, until these mental symptoms go away. Then, we are left with only mild symptoms like fatigue and brain fog. Once we reach a point where we spend little or no time each day worrying, these symptoms begin to clear up as well, signaling the end of the acute recovery period.

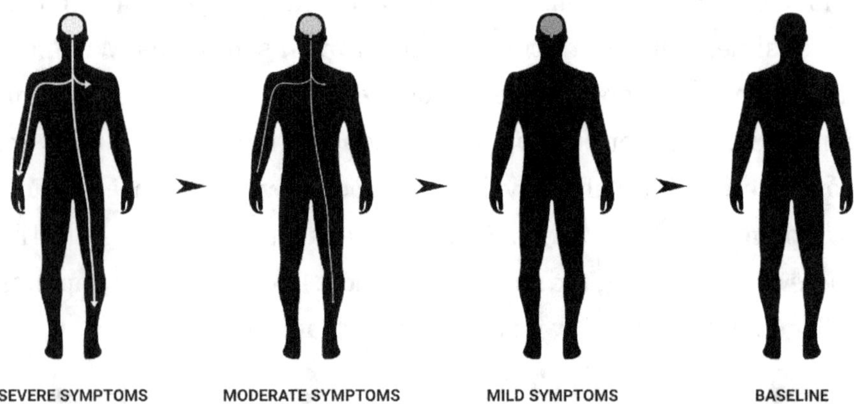

Symptoms gradually fading over the course of recovery.

At this stage, all that remains is to enjoy our hard-fought progress and keep practicing MBCT and CBT as needed.

Gauging Progress

While this view of adrenaline is helpful for understanding our recovery in the long term (over several months), we cannot use it to gauge our short-term progress (over a few days or weeks). This is because the body adjusts its production of adrenaline very slowly and gradually, and the day-to-day symptoms we experience will fluctuate based on factors like sleep, diet, activity levels, and even time of day.[85]

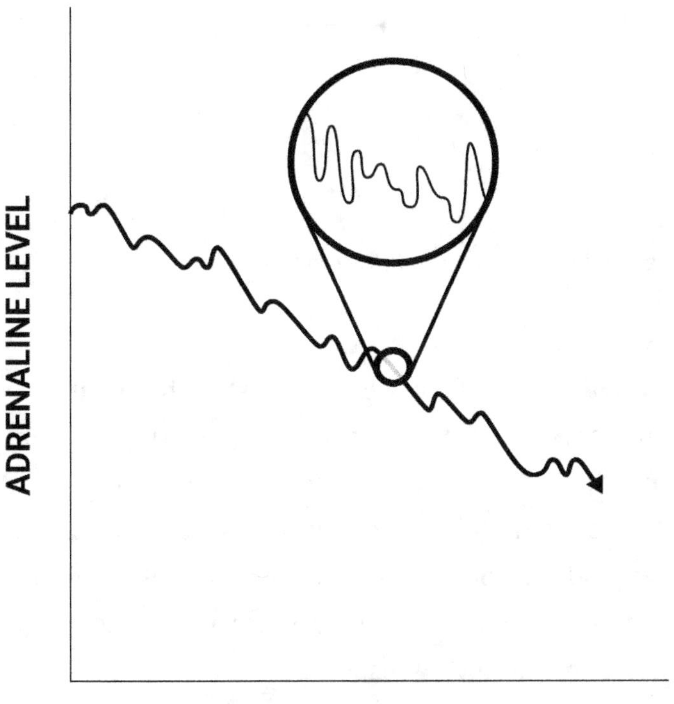

Adrenaline levels over the course of many months. Even when our adrenaline levels are decreasing, we will still experience daily fluctuations.

A much better way to gauge short-term progress is by looking at our response. As you can see in the figure below, the better we become at applying MBCT, the shorter and less intense our episodes of high adrenaline will be. Thus, rather than measuring our progress by how often symptoms appear, it is much better to measure how consistently we are applying MBCT.

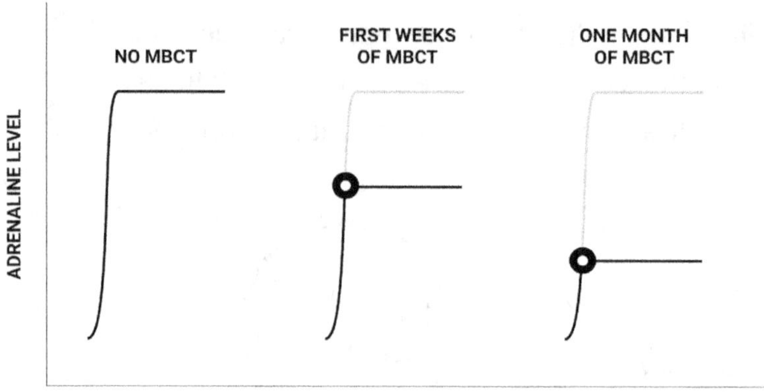

How episodes of high adrenaline look as we progress through MBCT.

Setbacks

While it would be ideal if recovery were a straightforward process, we are still human. Sometimes, we work on correcting one valuation for weeks, only to find that there is another one affecting us. Occasionally, we hit a cognitive blind spot and go back to worrying in ways we thought we had overcome. An old symptom might come back and the answer we used no longer works, or a new one comes up and it takes us time to figure out how to respond.

Small bumps in adrenaline will come and go, but there will come times when an unexpected event in our lives occurs—a health scare, a period of grief or discouragement, a big move—in which we will worry but feel too preoccupied to check our behavior. We may begin to worry excessively again, causing our adrenaline levels to go back up, leading old anxious symptoms to return and causing a **setback**.

If recovery is like a slow and gradual climb out of a hole, setbacks feel like getting thrown back in. They can come with flashbacks to our worst moments—causing suggestive thoughts like *What if that old symptom comes back even harder?* or *What if all of this progress was for nothing?* The first time we experience these thoughts, they are jarring, and since we are not used to responding to them, they can lead us to fall back even further.

As painful as setbacks may be, they serve an important purpose: to help us identify unhealthy valuations and cognitive blind spots. When we recognize ourselves worrying excessively—no matter if it is during a setback or not—it signals to us that one of our valuations is out of balance, *causing* us to worry and leading to those anxious symptoms.

When we notice this, our first job is to give context to our experience. We should ask ourselves if there was any event in our lives that drew our attention away from our response and led us to keep worrying. In addition, we should ask ourselves what about our response led us to behave this way—what valuation caused us to worry or what MBCT response was not working.

By doing so, we not only soften the blow of the setback, we find our way out of it; as we ask what we are worrying about and why (as in MBCT and CBT), we will eventually find our answer, allowing us to start progressing again. This is why, when we have these therapies at our side, *setbacks are always temporary.*

This is also why setbacks are always followed by huge progress. When we finally find the key to answering a suggestive thought—an aha moment where we realize how to move forward—we become able to build on our previous knowledge and future-proof ourselves against more worrying.

It is okay if you have difficulty internalizing this in your first couple setbacks. Once you have enough of them in the bag, you will start to see them for what they are: small road bumps on the greater path to recovery.

Full Recovery

I would like to leave off on a high note and discuss what full recovery looks like.

I have mentioned that recovering from a period of excessive worrying and high adrenaline is transformative, and now I will finally explain why.

Throughout our recovery, we will be introspective—asking ourselves questions about why we do what we do and how we can be better. We will enter situations, knowing we will be uncomfortable but choosing to work through them anyway. And we will do these things consistently over the course of many months and years.

Practicing these skills is so transformative because they are used in so many areas of our lives outside of mental health—being honestly introspective is what enables us to maintain healthy relationships and move past plateaus in our career. Being able to consistently confront discomfort and push through enables us to maintain a tough exercise regimen or a strict diet. And doing all of these consistently leads to a much better quality of life in the long term.

This is why so many people who overcome a period of high adrenaline find themselves achieving things they felt they never could: finding someone they truly love, finding satisfaction in their jobs, running a marathon, or finally losing the weight they had for their entire lives.

Of course, full recovery also comes with the benefit of no longer regularly experiencing anxious symptoms. When we first start on our journey to recovery, almost every moment can be spent nauseated, dissociated, and experiencing intrusive thoughts. But once we have fully recovered, our daily adrenaline levels will be low enough that we do not regularly experience any symptoms.

This is what life looks like for myself and everyone else who has recovered—we can find genuine pleasure in eating, socializing, and engaging with our work without being interrupted by frequent rushes of adrenaline. And in the exceedingly rare cases that our adrenaline does peak, we know how to act so that it goes away just as quickly.

Occasionally, we hit a setback, where we begin to worry like we used to, causing our adrenaline levels to rise for a few days or weeks. But after so much practice, we know how to handle it, and within a few days of identifying the problem, we return to baseline.

If you are currently lost in the dark and having difficulty seeing the light at the end of the tunnel, know that it is there. You are on the right path, and things will continue to get better as you keep searching for answers.

Conclusion

If you have made it to the end of this book, congratulations. You now have all of the knowledge and tools to pave your own path to recovery. It will be a long journey, one with many ups and downs, setbacks and leaps forward. But it is all for the sake of a better you. Many months from now, when your anxious symptoms and urges are just an afterthought, you will be able to look back and be proud of the work you did confronting a lifetime of unhealthy habits and having the strength to change them.

Now that we have reached the end, it is time for you to take everything you have learned and put it into action. Thank you for reading *The Anxiety Encyclopedia*, and I wish you luck on your journey.

Recommended Reading

Below is a list of books I recommend, separated by content.

Therapy Methods

The DARE Response by Barry McDonagh (MBCT): This is one of my personal favorites and my inspiration for writing this book. *The DARE Response* is a mix of MBCT, lifestyle changes, and personal development. I like Barry's work so much because his writing is warm. Not only does he give you the techniques to succeed, he writes about how to be kinder and more gentle with yourself, something I and many others often have trouble with.

Hope and Help for Your Nerves by Claire Weekes (MBCT): Claire Weekes is known as the mother of MBCT. Several of the most prolific authors about worrying and anxious symptoms draw inspiration from her, including Barry McDonagh. I would recommend reading through *The DARE Response* first, as it is simpler and more pleasant, and if you feel like you need more, try this book.

Feeling Good: The New Mood Therapy by David D. Burns (CBT): This book, written in the '80s and then updated a few decades later, is considered the gold standard for CBT. Burns does a deep dive into the most common cognitive distortions he has come across in his decades of therapy work, giving plenty of case studies and walking you through exactly how they recovered. You can read the book straight through if you want, but it was meant as more of a reference tool—you pick what distortion you are having the most trouble with and read through that chapter.

Lifestyle

*The Subtle Art of Not Giving a F*ck* by Mark Manson: This is another one of my personal favorites. Mark Manson's book includes a lot of the teachings of Buddhism but in a way that is much more digestible, interesting, and practical than the ancient art itself. It is a book about how sometimes life sucks, and how the healthiest thing we can do is embrace it. He reminds us that everyone has problems and whatever crisis we are going through at the moment, someone else has solved it and come out the other side. He reminds us there is nothing unique or special about our problems, and that is a good thing because it means we are just like everyone else—capable of getting better. If you are looking for some tough love, this may be the book for you. If you do not think you are quite at that stage yet, I think this book makes for a great read later on in treatment.

One warning: Manson has a discussion about OCD in which he calls it a "genetic condition" that can "only be managed and never cured." As you now know, this was a common misconception at the time this was written. However, I think the takeaway from his discussion on OCD, learning that we always have a sense of agency, is still just as valuable.

The AntiDepressant Solution: A Step-by-Step Guide to Safely Overcoming Antidepressant Withdrawal, Dependence, and Addiction by Dr. Joseph Glenmullen: Many of you reading this book will be taking an antidepressant and, after making improvement through the different therapies, will think about stopping. It is important to note that, because antidepressants induce withdrawal, we must take two precautions before choosing to stop. First, we must be under the supervision of a psychiatrist. Withdrawal causes unexpected symptoms, and having an experienced third party can help us answer suggestive thoughts.

Second, we have to slowly taper off of the medication because stopping antidepressants abruptly can bring much more serious and drawn-out withdrawal symptoms. Joseph Glenmullen's book has plenty of ideas for how to taper—both for antidepressant users and their doctors—so I highly recommend it.

Special Thanks

Thank you to those closest to me who helped me author this book and supported me throughout the writing process.

***Joe Bryer**, my original editor who put countless hours into making this book readable.*

*My therapist **Ms. Dana Eyal** and psychiatrist **Dr. Yuko Matsunaga**.*

***Christopher Chen**, illustrator of all figures you see in this book. Available at christopherchen.cc.*

***Matt Vachon**, photographer of my author's picture and designer of my website.
Available at mattvachon.com.*

***Michael Ponce**, designer of the cover art.
Available at behance.net/ponce.*

Thanks as well to:

Eric Parra

Joshua Lent Lipton

Ethan Lipton

Shahdad Rahimian

Matt Yamodim

References

Preface and Introduction

1   Statistics on anxiety

Facts & Statistics. Anxiety and Depression Association of America. Accessed October 11, 2020. https://adaa.org/about-adaa/press-room/facts-statistics

2   Trends in individuals experiencing anxious symptoms

Duffy ME, Twenge JM, Joiner TE. Trends in mood and anxiety symptoms and suicide-related outcomes among U.S. undergraduates, 2007–2018: evidence from two national surveys. *J Adolesc Health*. 2019;65(5):590-598. doi: 10.1016/j.jadohealth.2019.04.033

Biology

3   The amygdala's input/output system

LeDoux J. *Anxious: Using the Brain to Understand and Treat Fear and Anxiety*. Penguin Books; 2015:166.

4   The amygdala's creation of adrenaline

LeDoux J. *Anxious: Using the Brain to Understand and Treat Fear and Anxiety*. Penguin Books; 2015:60.

5   The effect of adrenaline on our blood vessels

Stress effects on the body. American Psychological Association. November 1, 2018. Accessed October 11, 2020. https://www.apa.org/helpcenter/stress-body

6   Anxious symptoms in animals

Tiiraab K, Sulkama S, Lohi H. Prevalence, comorbidity, and behavioral variation in canine anxiety. *J Vet Behav*. 2016;16:36-44. doi: 10.1016/j.jveb.2016.06.008

Ferdowsian HR, Durham DL, Kimwele C, et al. Signs of mood and anxiety disorders in chimpanzees. *PLoS One*. 2011;6(6):e19855. doi: 10.1371/journal.pone.0019855

Driscoll P, Fernàndez-Teruel A, Corda MG, Giorgi O, Steimer T. Some guidelines for defining personality differences in rats. In: Kim Y, ed. *Handbook of Behavior Genetics*. Springer; 2009:281-300. https://link.springer.com/book/10.1007/978-0-387-76727-7

7   The function of the emotional brain

LeDoux J. *Anxious: Using the Brain to Understand and Treat Fear and Anxiety*. Penguin Books; 2015:20.

8   Sense- and memory-related thoughts from the emotional brain

LeDoux J. *Anxious: Using the Brain to Understand and Treat Fear and Anxiety*. Penguin Books; 2015:254.

9   Reactionary behaviors from the emotional brain

LeDoux J. *Anxious: Using the Brain to Understand and Treat Fear and Anxiety*. Penguin Books; 2015:108.

10   The psychology of decision-making

Domenech P, Koechlin E. Executive control and decision-making in the prefrontal cortex. *Curr Opin Behav Sci*. 2015;1:101-106. doi: 10.1016/j.cobeha.2014.10.007

11   The orders of higher-level thinking

LeDoux J. *Anxious: Using the Brain to Understand and Treat Fear and Anxiety*. Penguin Books; 2015:160.

12   Synaptic pathways and the ease of decision making

Fuchs E, Flügge G. Adult neuroplasticity: more than 40 years of research. *Neural Plast*. 2014;2014:541870. doi: 10.1155/2014/541870

Schaffer J. Neuroplasticity and clinical practice: building brain power for health. *Front Psychol*. 2016;7:1118. doi: 10.3389/fpsyg.2016.01118

13   The energizing of the emotional brain

LeDoux J. *Anxious: Using the Brain to Understand and Treat Fear and Anxiety*. Penguin Books; 2015:97.

14   How worrying causes anxious symptoms

Lebow MA, Chen A. Overshadowed by the amygdala: the bed nucleus of the stria terminalis emerges as key to psychiatric disorders. *Mol Psychiatry*. 2016;21(4):450-463. doi: 10.1038/mp.2016.1

LeDoux J. *Anxious: Using the Brain to Understand and Treat Fear and Anxiety*. Penguin Books; 2015:15.

15   Physical symptoms of worrying

Jennings JR, Hall SW Jr. Recall, recognition, and rate: memory and heart. *Psychophysiology*. 1980;17(1):37-46. doi: 10.1111/j.1469-8986.1980.tb02457.x

Zingaretti P, Giovanardi G, Cruciani G, Lingiardi V, Ottaviani C, Spitoni GF. Heart rate variability in response to the recall of attachment memories. *Attach Hum Dev*. 2019 Oct 24;1-10. doi: 10.1080/14616734.2019.1680712

van der Wel P, van Steenbergen H. Pupil dilation as an index of effort in cognitive control tasks: a review. *Psychon Bull Rev*. 2018;25(6):2005-2015. doi: 10.3758/s13423-018-1432-y

16 Neuroplasticity

Fuchs E, Flügge G. Adult neuroplasticity: more than 40 years of research. *Neural Plast*. 2014;2014:541870. doi: 10.1155/2014/541870

17 Retention of neuroplasticity throughout our lives

Pauwels L, Chalavi S, Swinnen SP. Aging and brain plasticity. *Aging (Albany NY)*. 2018;10(8):1789-1790. doi: 10.18632/aging.101514

18 Sensitization of the amygdala

LeDoux J. *Anxious: Using the Brain to Understand and Treat Fear and Anxiety*. Penguin Books; 2015:27.

19 Effects of genetics on amygdala sensitization

LeDoux J. *Anxious: Using the Brain to Understand and Treat Fear and Anxiety*. Penguin Books; 2015:28.

20 Situational sensitivity of the amygdala

LeDoux J. *Anxious: Using the Brain to Understand and Treat Fear and Anxiety*. Penguin Books; 2015:28, 270.

21 Extinction of the emotional brain

LeDoux J. *Anxious: Using the Brain to Understand and Treat Fear and Anxiety*. Penguin Books; 2015:68.

22 Adopting valuations based on our surroundings

LeDoux J. *Anxious: Using the Brain to Understand and Treat Fear and Anxiety*. Penguin Books; 2015:16.

23 Overvaluation of distrust and self-criticism in helicopter families

Effects of child abuse and neglect. Joyful Heart Foundation. Accessed October 11, 2020. http://www.joyfulheartfoundation.org/learn/child-abuse-neglect/effects-child-abuse-neglect

24 How our valuations stray from reality

Rudolph KD, Clark AG. Conceptions of relationships in children with depressive and aggressive symptoms: social-cognitive distortion or reality? *J Abnorm Child Psychol*. 2001;29(1):41-56. doi: 10.1023/a:1005299429060

25 Prevalence of anxious symptoms in those with stressful jobs

Avgoustaki A, Frankort H. Working long and hard? It may do more harm than good. Cass Business School. September 6, 2018. Accessed October 11, 2020. https://www.cass.city.ac.uk/news-and-events/news/2018/september/working-long-and-hard-it-may-do-more-harm-than-good

26 Symptoms of panic

Panic disorder. NHS. Reviewed July 28, 2020. Accessed October 11, 2020. https://www.nhs.uk/conditions/panic-disorder/

27 Typical length of panic

Bandelow B, Domschke K, Baldwin DS. *Panic Disorder and Agoraphobia.* Oxford University Press; 2014.

28 Amygdala conditioning in phobias

LeDoux J. *Anxious: Using the Brain to Understand and Treat Fear and Anxiety.* Penguin Books; 2015:110.

29 Most common phobias

Cherry K. 10 of the most common phobias. Verywell Mind. Updated January 20, 2020. Accessed October 11, 2020. https://www.verywellmind.com/most-common-phobias-4136563

30 Strengthening of compulsions

Luigjes J, Lorenzetti V, de Haan S. Defining compulsive behavior. *Neuropsychol Rev.* 2019;29(1):4-13. doi: 10.1007/s11065-019-09404-9

31 Overlap between obsessive urges, worrying, and anxious symptoms

Luigjes J, Lorenzetti V, de Haan S. Defining compulsive behavior. *Neuropsychol Rev.* 2019;29(1):4-13. doi: 10.1007/s11065-019-09404-9

32 Shortcomings of antidepressants

Moncrieff J, Kirsch I. Efficacy of antidepressants in adults. *BMJ.* 2005;331(7509):155-157. doi: 10.1136/bmj.331.7509.155

33 Weak connection between genetics and panic/worrying/obsessive urges

Eley TC, McAdams TA, Rijsdijk FV. The intergenerational transmission of anxiety: a children-of-twins study. *Am J Psychiatry.* 2015;172(7):630-637. doi: 10.1176/appi.ajp.2015.14070818

34 Effect of weight loss on weight-related illnesses

Hallberg SJ, Gershuni VM, Hazbun TL, Athinarayanan SJ. Reversing type 2 diabetes: a narrative review of the evidence. *Nutrients.* 2019;11(4):766. doi: 10.3390/nu11040766

MBCT

35 Barry McDonagh on stopping techniques

McDonagh B. *Dare: The New Way to End Anxiety and Stop Panic Attacks.* Dare People Pty; 2015:14.

36 The body's ability to dispense of adrenaline as quickly as it needs to

Adrenaline (Epinephrine) Injection BP 1 in 1000. Prescribing information. Hameln Pharma Ltd; 1978. Accessed October 11, 2020. https://www.medicines.org.uk/emc/product/6284/smpc

37 Unconscious control over breathing

Mitchell GS, Baker-Herman TL, McCrimmon DR, Feldman JL. Respiration. In: Squire LR, ed. *Encyclopedia of Neuroscience.* Elsevier; 2009:121-130.

38 Tingling sensation when relaxing out of fight or flight

How stress affects your feet. Texas Foot & Ankle Center. Accessed October 11, 2020. https://txfac.com/blog/how-stress-affects-your-feet/

39 Prevalence of cardiovascular disease in the US

Heart disease. CDC. Reviewed June 23, 2020. Updated October 11, 2020. https://www.cdc.gov/heartdisease/

40 Mechanism of a heart attack

Heart attack. Mayo Clinic. June 16, 2020. Accessed October 11, 2020. https://www.mayoclinic.org/diseases-conditions/heart-attack/symptoms-causes/syc-20373106

41 Harmlessness of heart palpitations

Heart palpitations and ectopic beats. NHS. Reviewed October 24 2019. Accessed October 11, 2020. https://www.nhs.uk/conditions/heart-palpitations

42 Heart rate as a measure of workout productivity

Exercise intensity. Better Health Channel. Updated June 2015. Accessed October 11, 2020. https://www.betterhealth.vic.gov.au/health/HealthyLiving/exercise-intensity

43 Adrenaline's effect on swallowing

Lee BE, Kim GH. Globus pharyngeus: A review of its etiology, diagnosis and treatment. *World J Gastroenterol.* 2012;18(20):2462-2471. doi: 10.3748/wjg.v18.i20.2462

44 Barry McDonagh on the actual symptoms of throat cancer

McDonagh B. *Dare: The New Way to End Anxiety and Stop Panic Attacks.* Dare People Pty; 2015:101.

45 Blood being drawn away from extremities in fight or flight

Raypole C. Feeling numb or tingly? It might be anxiety. Healthline. June 2, 2020. Accessed October 11, 2020. https://www.healthline.com/health/anxiety-numbness

46 Numbness and tingling in other conditions

Diabetic neuropathy. Mayo Clinic. March 03, 2020. Accessed October 11, 2020. https://www.mayoclinic.org/diseases-conditions/diabetic-neuropathy/symptoms-causes/syc-20371580

47 Temporary effects of short-term sleep loss vs long-term

Zhao Z, Zhao X, Veasey SC. Neural consequences of chronic short sleep: reversible or lasting? *Front Neurol.* 2017;8:235. doi: 10.3389/fneur.2017.00235

48 Barry McDonagh on sleeping

McDonagh B. *Dare: The New Way to End Anxiety and Stop Panic Attacks.* Dare People Pty; 2015:138.

49 Definition of hypnic jerks

Holland K. Twitching before falling asleep: what causes hypnic jerks? Healthline. Updated November 12, 2019. Accessed October 11, 2020. https://www.healthline.com/health/hypnagogic-jerk

50 Mechanism of hypnic jerks

Castro J. Why do people 'twitch' when falling asleep? Live Science. November 21, 2017. Accessed October 11, 2020. https://www.livescience.com/39225-why-people-twitch-falling-asleep.html

51 Vertigo tests in the doctor's office

Labuguen RH. Initial evaluation of vertigo. *Am Fam Physician.* 2006;73(2):244-51.

52 Fainting due to drop in blood pressure

Syncope (fainting). American Heart Association. Reviewed June 30, 2017. Accessed October 11, 2020. https://www.heart.org/en/health-topics/arrhythmia/symptoms-diagnosis--monitoring-of-arrhythmia/syncope-fainting

53 Fainting due to dehydration

When should you worry about fainting? Harvard Health Publishing. July 2015. Updated September 10, 2019. Accessed October 11, 2020. https://www.health.harvard.edu/diseases-and-conditions/when-should-you-worry-about-fainting

54 Role of neck muscles in balance

Anthony K. Cervical vertigo. Healthline. Updated September 28, 2018. Accessed October 11, 2020. https://www.healthline.com/health/cervical-vertigo

55 Interaction of adrenaline with the vestibular system

Cervicogenic headache. American Migraine Foundation. October 24, 2016. Accessed October 11, 2020. https://americanmigrainefoundation.org/resource-library/cervicogenic-headache

56 Neck weakness as a cause of migraine-like headaches

Cervicogenic headache. American Migraine Foundation. October 24, 2016. Accessed October 11, 2020. https://americanmigrainefoundation.org/resource-library/cervicogenic-headache

57 Neck stretches for headaches

How to stretch your neck. WebMD. Reviewed January 26, 2020. Accessed October 11, 2020. https://www.webmd.com/fitness-exercise/fitness-neck-stretches

58 Posture recommendations for neck strength

Common posture mistakes and fixes. NHS. Reviewed July 10, 2019. Accessed October 11, 2020. https://www.nhs.uk/live-well/exercise/common-posture-mistakes-and-fixes

59 Dehydration headaches

O'Keefe Osborn C. Recognizing a dehydration headache. Healthline. Updated August 12, 2019. Accessed October 11, 2020. https://www.healthline.com/health/dehydration-headache

60 Treatability of all kinds of headaches

Headaches: treatment depends on your diagnosis and symptoms. Mayo Clinic. May 10, 2019. Accessed October 11, 2020. https://www.mayoclinic.org/diseases-conditions/chronic-daily-headaches/in-depth/headaches/art-20047375

61 Hyper-awareness of the emotional brain

LeDoux J. *Anxious: Using the Brain to Understand and Treat Fear and Anxiety.* Penguin Books; 2015:109

62 Eye floaters

Eye floaters: causes, symptoms, and treatment. WebMD. Reviewed March 30, 2019. Accessed October 11, 2020. https://www.webmd.com/eye-health/benign-eye-floaters

63 Sexual dysfunction as a result of adrenaline

Holland K. Can stress and anxiety cause erectile dysfunction? Healthline. Updated July 1, 2017. Accessed October 11, 2020. https://www.healthline.com/health/erectile-dysfunction-anxiety-stress

64 Other causes of sexual dysfunction

Erectile dysfunction. Mayo Clinic. March 27, 2020. Accessed October 11, 2020. https://www.mayoclinic.org/diseases-conditions/erectile-dysfunction/symptoms-causes/syc-20355776

65 Mechanism of depersonalization

Michal M, Koechel A, Canterino M, et al. Depersonalization disorder: disconnection of cognitive evaluation from autonomic responses to emotional stimuli. *PLoS One*. 2013;8(9):e74331. doi: 10.1371/journal.pone.0074331

66 Number of thoughts our emotional brain creates each day

Tseng J, Poppenk J. Brain meta-state transitions demarcate thoughts across task contexts exposing the mental noise of trait neuroticism. *Nat Commun*. 2020;11(1):3480. doi: 10.1038/s41467-020-17255-9

67 "If you think you are going crazy, you probably aren't"

McDonagh B. *Dare: The New Way to End Anxiety and Stop Panic Attacks*. Dare People Pty; 2015:10.

68 Developmental theory of schizophrenia

Fatemi SH, Folsom TD. The neurodevelopmental hypothesis of schizophrenia, revisited. *Schizophr Bull*. 2009;35(3):528-548. doi: 10.1093/schbul/sbn187

69 Lack of awareness in patients with aggressive psychotic illness

Gilleen J, Greenwood K, David AS. Domains of awareness in schizophrenia. *Schizophr Bull*. 2011;37(1):61-72. doi: 10.1093/schbul/sbq100

70 Diagnosis of psychotic illnesses

Mental health screening. MedlinePlus. Updated February 26, 2020. Accessed October 11, 2020. https://medlineplus.gov/lab-tests/mental-health-screening

71 Long-term success in treatment of psychotic illness

Larsen-Barr M, Seymour F, Read J, Gibson K. Attempting to discontinue antipsychotic medication: withdrawal methods, relapse and success. *Psychiatry Res*. 2018;270:365-374. doi: 10.1016/j.psychres.2018.10.001

72 Mechanism of brain fog

Ocon AJ. Caught in the thickness of brain fog: exploring the cognitive symptoms of chronic fatigue syndrome. *Front Physiol*. 2013;4:63. doi: 10.3389/fphys.2013.00063

73 Emotional numbing during a period of high adrenaline

Gotter A. Understanding emotional numbness. Healthline. Updated September 17, 2018. Accessed October 11, 2020. https://www.healthline.com/health/feeling-numb

ERP

74 Direct ERP's effect on the brain

LeDoux J. *Anxious: Using the Brain to Understand and Treat Fear and Anxiety.* Penguin Books; 2015:264.

Lifestyle

75 Benefits of exercise

Benefits of exercise. NHS. Reviewed June 11, 2018. Accessed October 11, 2020. https://www.nhs.uk/live-well/exercise/exercise-health-benefits

76 Mechanism of dehydration

Bouby N, Fernandes S. Mild dehydration, vasopressin and the kidney: animal and human studies. *Eur J Clin Nutr.* 2003;57(Suppl 2):S39-S46. doi: 10.1038/sj.ejcn.1601900

77 Effect of caffeine on blood pressure

Coffee and your blood pressure. Harvard Health Publishing. March 2014. Updated April 3, 2019. Accessed October 11, 2020. https://www.health.harvard.edu/heart-health/coffee_and_your_blood_pressure

78 Benefits of meditation

Thorpe M. 12 science-based benefits of meditation. Healthline. July 5, 2017. Accessed October 11, 2020. https://www.healthline.com/nutrition/12-benefits-of-meditation

79 Effect of lack of sleep on blood pressure

Doyle CY, Ruiz JM, Taylor DJ, et al. Associations between objective sleep and ambulatory blood pressure in a community sample. *Psychosom Med.* 2019;81(6):545-556. doi: 10.1097/psy.0000000000000711

80 Light exposure and production of sleep hormones

Blue light has a dark side. Harvard Health Publishing. May 2012. Updated July 7, 2020. Accessed October 11, 2020. https://www.health.harvard.edu/staying-healthy/blue-light-has-a-dark-side

81 Effect of social media on long-term mood

Berry N, Emsley R, Lobban F, Bucci S. Social media and its relationship with mood, self-esteem and paranoia in psychosis. *Acta Psychiatr Scand.* 2018;138(6):558-570. doi: 10.1111/acps.12953

82 Advantages of optimism over pessimism

Optimism and your health. Harvard Health Publishing. May 2008. Accessed October 11, 2020. https://www.health.harvard.edu/heart-health/optimism-and-your-health

83 Effect of CBT on long-term mood

Veddegjaerde KE. Long term effect of cognitive behavioral therapy in patients with health anxiety. *Eur Psychiatry.* 2017;41(Suppl):S111-S112. doi: 10.1016/j.eurpsy.2017.01.1887

84 Difficulty maintaining resolutions

New Year's resolution project. Quirkology. Accessed October 11, 2020. http://www.richardwiseman.com/quirkology/new/USA/Experiment_resolution.shtml

85 Fluctuations of adrenaline throughout the day

Dodt C, Breckling U, Derad I, Fehm HL, Born J. Plasma epinephrine and norepinephrine concentrations of healthy humans associated with night-time sleep and morning arousal. *Hypertension.* 1997;30(1 Pt 1):71-76. doi: 10.1161/01.hyp.30.1.71

www.ingramcontent.com/pod-product-compliance
Lightning Source LLC
Chambersburg PA
CBHW061342250726
48657CB00004B/1295